I DIDN'T KNOW WHAT TO SAY

Being A Better Friend to
Those Who Experience Loss

David Knapp

I DIDN'T KNOW WHAT TO SAY:
Being A Better Friend to Those Who Experience Loss
By David Knapp

Printed in the United States of America

ISBN 978-0-692-47880-6

Cover designed by Robert Gibson
Square1 Media Group

Dedication

This book is dedicated to women in my life who have influenced me greatly in who I am today, with much appreciation.

Merle Stanton Jones *(grandmother)*

Merilee Jones Knapp Parker *(mother)*

Ruth Cox Knapp *(wife)*

Judith Willard Schiffner Knapp *(wife)*

Table of Contents

Foreword

Every country and culture exhibits traditions and procedures for dealing with loss. These practices range from how to respond to death all the way up to how a group acts when they have lost a beloved leader or governmental power control. Often the social responses to loss are passed on in non-verbal ways while other times there is clear protocol included in the laws of the land or community on the topic.

On a personal level, people everywhere experience loss as a normal part of life. Some losses actually stimulate growth or progress. Whether it be a toddler learning to walk, or an athlete losing a game, loss often motivates. The loss of privileges can be an effective form of discipline parents often use to mold their children into responsible adults.

Learning how to be a better friend to someone who has experienced loss may require a close look at our own understanding about loss. Our tendency is to respond to others based on our own experiences and through our own grid. If our thinking needs correcting, the natural result will be for us to pass our inaccuracies about the topic on in what we say to others.

Much of the material available on this topic is written to reflect on grief itself and give guidance to the griever.

However, not as much instruction is out there to help those who want to be assistance in times of loss.

Each of us will find ourselves in a position of potentially being that friend or relative with the task of having input into the life and experience of someone we know and love who has experienced a loss of some kind. As part of their circle of influence, we can play an important role in helping them process their grief with victory.

We often do not know what to do in times of others' loss. Sometimes we are simply silent. Sometimes we may avoid the person. Other times, we may try to help by using logic. It becomes clear that we often do not know what to say. We feel uncomfortable.

For some, grief due to loss creates a reality check. Life and circumstances come into a new focus with trite values fading into the shadows. At such times as these, it can be of great benefit to have friends in one's life who understand and know what to say, or not say, that could assist in gaining or regaining a stable grip on what is true and beneficial.

You will find this handbook on what to say and not say to those who have experienced loss very practical as well as realistic. Learning from the experiences of those who have "been there, done that" to have an improved grasp on the grieving process will provide a basis to formulate statements of hope and comfort for your friends and relatives.

Don Stephens
President and Founder
Mercy Ships

Introduction

Nobody really wants to experience loss, pain, heart-ache, disappointment, grief or mourning. The truth, however, emerges that they are all a part of human existence. These things will happen to all of us at some point. Beginning with the loss of the safe, warm environment of the womb until the news that one will soon lose their physical life, our journey contains various levels and degrees of loss.

Adjusting to loss seems to be a core issue in life. Whether it is the childish horror of a toddler losing their blanket or a child relinquishing their position as baby of the family to a new addition, loss requires confrontation. Every one of us will experience the emotional hurt from grief caused by the loss or death of someone or something they are close to. How do you cope?

My experiences with loss may seem like an unusual amount to some people. However, I'm reminded of the story about the man who was the sole survivor of the Johnstown Flood. During his life he bragged a lot about that distinction. Upon arriving in heaven he began his boasting until someone said, "So, there is someone here you need to meet. His name is Noah." Yes, there will always be someone who has gone through more. So, I don't waste time with pity parties.

As you will read, my first devastating encounter with grief came through the death of my wife. I was in my late 30s, administrator and teacher at a college and parenting four young children. I didn't know a human could hurt that much. It was all so new to me and I had no idea that some of my viewpoints about deep mourning were so off base. The "hole in my soul" haunted me.

My experience of going through grief did more than temporarily affect my life. I became a student of what was going on in (not easy for this man) and around me. I observed how those around me reacted to the same event and how they responded to me. Few seemed to have any better grasp of grief than I had. The knowledge I gained from my research soon began to drive me to reach out and help others experiencing loss in ways no one did for me.

One of the dominant methods of dealing with grief and loss of others is avoidance. Our default ways of coping with grief tend to be to change the subject, stuff it down, explain it away, prevent grief's symptoms or try to get over it or away quickly. Since grief feels so uncomfortable, sidestepping is our first reaction.

My studies of the grieving process showed me that grief was not only normal, but required. This also applies to those who make up a support circle around the griever. Grief is as natural as bleeding when you cut your arm and time and attention is needed to heal. Ignoring the cut can lead to infection, just like thwarted grief can cause issues in one's life, whether evident immediately or later. Some cuts require the aid of others to properly deal with and often, grief is best processed with the help of friends or relatives.

I wanted to be that better friend to people in my life who go through the grieving process.

Then came the death of my second wife twenty-two years later. The lessons I had gathered from my first wife's death were unavoidably refreshed. My notes and observations took on a deeper, more refined form.

More than one friend admitted to me, *"I didn't know what to say."* When we'd talk and I explained to them what it was like in the grieving process and how I could have been helped, their responses were so positive. I sensed a deep compulsion inside me, *"Don't hoard your lessons."* Requests for written versions of my story and lessons mounted. I began to see that most people, whether friends or family or in professional capacities, really did want to connect with a person in grief, but fear, ignorance or verbal clumsiness held them back. And just like First-Aid 101, there were things that could be learned.

My professional background includes that of being a teacher. You will find that showing through in the following pages as I share practical suggestions for dealing with varying kinds of loss. For the hurried reader, there are even lists that should be helpful. All this springs from the lessons learned through my experiences. It is true that those who are in the throes of grieving will find help in the revealing portrayal of my own personal grieving experiences. However, my dominant objective for writing my story is to help the rest of us be a better friend to those who are grieving.

"The friend who can be silent with us in a moment of despair or confusion, who can stay with us in an hour of grief and bereavement, who can tolerate not knowing ... not healing, not curing ... that is a friend who cares."

HENRI NOUWEN

Chapter 1

—

WHEN I EXPERIENCED LOSS

My life lived through
multiple losses

I didn't know a human could hurt so much.

It's not like I had never experienced loss. My grandfather died when I was six. I remember the event and the emotions of others but I did not feel devastated. I do however, remember Mom's pain when Dad was killed in a farming accident; I was 11, the eldest of four children. Mom's grieving was compounded by the birth of my youngest brother one week after Dad's funeral on a bleak February day. Baby by her side, she cried in bed most of the time, for a long time. Still, my pain was not soul wrenching. I don't remember crying, but all I really recall was the constant reminder that he was no longer there. His chair sat empty at the head of the table haunting reminder of my uncle's first words after they took Dad's body away, "What a big responsibility for such a young boy." I had lost a dad and a leader. My only feelings were that of hollowness inside me and a sense of abandonment. He was gone.

Loss began to have more of an impact as I entered my teenage years. During high school I had a dog named Lady, who followed me everywhere possible. Although she may have been ugly to look at, there was no companion more loyal. When she was hit by a car and had to be relieved of her misery, it hurt. She was my best friend. I stood there watching her die and ached inside.

My first sense of deep loss as an adult came when a group of friends moved out of my life. I worked with a religious non-profit that specialized in developing teams. Quite naturally, after spending so much time together, we became very close. It was a sad day when they moved to another job assignment. Coincidentally, I listened to one member of our group say that one of the reasons she tried NOT to get close to team members is because it was so painful to her when it came time to say goodbye. To her, the loss was too deep. I didn't agree with her logic, but I understood.

The anguish that hit hardest in my life to that point, was the loss of my wife, Ruth, to cancer. It seemed so unfair that we were dealing with a life-threatening condition in our early thirties, but there we were. In a way, we began grieving our losses the day we received the horrid diagnosis. Ruth would not see our four children graduate from high school, she'd miss knowing her grandkids and our long-term dreams were gone – vanished. Future years of service together became a fantasy. Due to her treatments our normal life became elusive, and so it went. All this pain accumulated in addition to her possible physical death in a yet-to-be determined time frame. We set out on an intentional path to live life to the fullest in all possible ways.

Seven years of treatment, surgeries, tears and hopes suddenly came to an abrupt end the moment I watched her take her last breath. I mumbled a broken, "*Goodbye...Ruth,*" and collapsed into a sobbing heap in my chair. The shock was more soul-wrenching than anything I had ever experienced. I didn't know a human could hurt so much. Her death was somehow a shock because I had clutched to hope for a few more months with her.

The following months took me through a mourning process that was foreign to me. Even though I had been blessed with a great circle of friends, an amazing team at work, caring members from the church we attended and a dedicated family, I still experienced profound feelings of loss and emptiness. Agonizing loneliness, devastating longing, missing my best friend and lover occupied my every moment. I found myself wandering around the house like a toddler looking for his pacifier.

One of the things that struck me as odd was the huge variety of ways people attempted to talk to me in the early weeks after my wife's death, followed by a complete lack of conversation about her or my loss in the weeks to come. It was as if she had never been. Often-times I realized that the way people responded to my loss revolved more around their need instead of mine. A few who had experienced their own losses got it right. Precious few admitted they *"Didn't know what to say."*

People began pulling away from me after about the third week following her funeral, while my need to talk only increased. In truth, I would have given anything for someone to ask me, *"Could you tell me about your wife's death?"* But no one ever asked.

Consequently, I began an intentional effort to find others who may have experienced a similar loss so I could talk about my experience and work through my pain. One motive for seeking out others was to comfort them through listening and understanding their heart-felt exchanges, while fulfilling my need to share concerning my own loss and process of grief. This part of my grieving process continued for six months after my wife's death. By the end of this period I had either forgotten or gotten over the negative effects caused by those who said the wrong thing to me during my grief period.

Working through the loss of my wife left me stronger. I remember thinking that nothing else in life could be harder. The deep pain had left my feelings for others' hurts closer to the surface.

Fortunately, the year after Ruth's death I met a wonderful widowed lady. Mutual friends actually talked her into attending the college where I was teaching so we would meet. It certainly took nerve for her to do that. This "arranged" and seemingly innocent meeting allowed me to easily be drawn to her. You see, Judith was the most beautiful lady I had met in a long time. It was love at first sight. That next year we were married.

The day we married my four children were in their teens and Judith's four boys were also teens. Yes, we blended eight teenagers into a family and survived. Telling that success story must be left for another day.

I could not foresee the heavy challenge emerging the year after our marriage. A policy of the religious non-profit organization with whom I worked forced my resignation from the group, against my wishes! I involuntarily left my leadership position and a 20-year career. This sudden unemployment hit me harder than a blow to the stomach. I had never experienced such depth of rejection before.

Losing my position and the relationships I'd cultivated with co-workers turned into an emotional nightmare for me. Part of the reason for the inner turmoil occurred because I failed to recognize these losses as something to be dealt with in a "grieving" fashion. I just sucked it up, acted brave about the whole situation and moved on to a new job. WRONG!

Only Judith really saw the sinking spirit in me during the next three years. She understood my silent grieving. But I pretty much suffered alone, not wanting her or the children to endure my sorrow. Occasionally while alone, I would experience sudden outbursts of grief. But I wrongly attributed those emotional bouts to residual grieving over my first wife's death. Not always so.

My strong faith in God provided the strength to continue.

The next 20 years contained many successes both through our work and family victories. Judith and I moved two more times in response to jobs and family duties, landing in Arizona following her mother's death.

The very next year we became concerned for Judith's health. We both sensed something was wrong but didn't want to consider the worst possibility. Five years of changing doctors, along with many tests finally exposed a large tumor on her pancreas. By the time doctors and tests exposed this culprit; time had run out for successful treatment.

Judith passed from this world victoriously the same month 22 years later as had my first wife.

Another deep mourning process began. Some asked if I found it easier or harder the second time. My answer? It was harder. We had only three months from prognosis to passing. During that time Judith and I intensely and intentionally mourned her impending death together. Plus, we invited each of our eight children and their families (24 grandkids) to come join me in saying "Goodbye" to their mother and grandmother. Each visit magnified the reality that Judith was leaving us and there was nothing we could do. The process hurt beyond imagination but it also played a huge part in all of our healing processes in the months to come.

As before, I was supported by a wonderful circle of friends and family. Our church group cared for us in great ways for more than three months and beyond. But just as before, even those expressions of support could not fill the empty soul-wrenching hurt in my spirit – I missed her. Only time and the grieving process would resolve the void her absence left in me.

This time, not only did I face an empty bed but also an empty house. The loneliness was deafening. And as before, I observed those who admitted to me honestly, they *"Didn't know what to say."*

In an effort to help the many friends and acquaintances who expressed this sentiment of well-meaning concern, I became very open when talking to friends about my grieving process. It became obvious that my explanations opened their understanding of the grieving experience, clarifying ways in which they could help me and others through their speech and actions.

I can only express what I know and have experienced. While I am a professional, I make no claims on having official training to deal with all people in all sorts of grief. My expressions come only from my own life and from conversations with others. I recommend that individuals who seem to be in physical and emotional states beyond common dialog, be referred to professional help.

My hope is that the following experiences and suggestions will be helpful to you as you aid co-workers, friends and family encounter who are experiencing their own losses. Perhaps something you find in the pages to follow will help you be a better friend or loved one in a time of grief.

◆

« Point To Ponder »

Comments of comfort should not be geared to "fix" the problem of grief for the bereaved.

FREE DOWNLOAD: The core theme of this book is knowing what to say to be of benefit to grievers as well as what NOT to say to them that might not be so helpful. For a complete list of the suggestions made in this book, click on the following link to access the handy PDF. What To Say, What Not To Say. http://bit.ly/HCOP90

WHAT TO SAY

WHAT NOT TO SAY

✓ **Your loss is a very difficult thing to go through, I am sure.**

    ✗ *Get a grip!*

✓ **I will always remember him/her.**

    ✗ *I don't want to talk about the dead. Let's talk about the living.*

✓ **Do you need someone to go with you to choose a casket or marker?**

    ✗ *I know what you are going through. I lost a kitten once.*

✓ **Can we go for a walk on Sunday afternoon and chat?**

    ✗ *You need to take your mind totally off your pain.*

✓ **Tell me something special about your early days with him/her.**

    ✗ *You should be thankful he/she is out of pain.*

"He that is thy friend indeed, he will help thee in thy need:
If thou sorrow, he will weep; if thou wake, he cannot sleep;
thus of every grief in heart he with thee doth bear a part."

RICHARD BARNFIELD

Chapter 2

—

WHEN MOURNING HAPPENS

Some of the basics about
the mourning process

What's wrong with me? It's like I have lost control of who I am.

Boy, did I have a lot to learn. My views about the process of grieving had to be overhauled. My erroneous views permeated the experience, attitude and thinking. I had to admit that the way I viewed grieving was all wrong. Instead of seeing the process as a means to added strength, I had seen it as weakness. But now when I hear an insightful or deep truth or concept, I wonder what loss the author experienced to learn that. Instead of seeing grieving as a process towards healing, I had concluded it to be an event to "get over."

One of the motivations I have for penning this book comes from the large number of people who have admitted to me that they "Didn't know what to say." Our society has collected huge volumes of information on how to aid others who experience physical problems from the common cold to a broken leg. However, when it comes to dealing with a broken heart we draw a blank and often pull away.

Yet our emotions are just as much a part of what it means to be alive as our physical bodies. Surely, life and loss require us to learn the skill of working through losses that can negatively affect how we feel in spirit.

HEART VS. MIND

Understanding a few of the basics about the grieving process (i.e. a broken heart) can go a long way in aiding us in knowing what to say to those who are encountering losses life throws at them. The list of losses that merit being classified as "grievable" is much larger than many would admit. The following compilation is far from complete, but it should broaden the scope of our understanding:

- Death of a spouse
- Death of a relative or friend
- Death or lost custody of a child
- Death of an cherished pet
- Marriage or Divorce
- Loss of a friendship

- Moving to a new community
- Stages of the "empty nest"
- Retirement
- Loss of a job or position
- Loss of health
- Major financial changes
- Addictions
- Legal problems
- Starting or finishing school

Some would look at my partial list and respond, "Well, isn't that all just a part of life?" Yes, it is. That's the point exactly. We all have and do experience loss as a part of everyday life. However, we don't always deal with the grieving process well. The negative effects of undealt with grief can be a hindrance to our emotions and spirit.

Misconceptions about the grieving process are diverse. Here are some I had to work through. I am sure you will relate to some of them.

GRIEVING IS NOT WRONG

My biggest misconception came from an attitude that grieving was negative and showed weakness. I would have to go so far as to say I viewed it as sin. One thing that may have contributed to this wrong attitude may have come from watching my well-meaning grandmother deal with my mom's mourning following my dad's death.

A major event happened without warning. Grandmother showed up at our house unannounced. As had been the situation for two weeks, my mom was still in bed in the middle of the day with a newborn at her breast. The house was a mess from the unattended activities of four other children. Instead of concern, my grandmother yelled at my mom requiring her to get out of bed and stop her grieving. She complied and that emotional event left an impression on my young heart that my mom was doing something wrong. (More in chapter 4.)

My grandmother could have accomplished the same thing by simply cleaning the house and then talking to my mother. She could have said comforting things like, "You must be really hurting inside right now. Let me help you so you can get back on your feet. Come sit in this chair and feed the baby while I make your bed."

GRIEVING IS NORMAL

Realizing that grieving is a normal and healthy response to loss set me free to embrace the process and accept the characteristics of mourning as okay and right. I am thankful for a couple of mentors who came along-side me after Ruth's death. They showed me the value of leaning into the process instead of resisting it. First I realized that grief is simply an emotional acknowledgement of loss. It is mostly a heart problem and not a mind challenge.

Cliché comments like, "You have to be strong" or "God doesn't give us more than we can bear" often feed the misconception that grieving is negative and wrong. Instead of implying folks struggle against their hurts, you can be more understanding with comments like, "I'm sorry this has happened to you" or "You must hurt (or miss them) very much right now."

PEOPLE GRIEVE DIFFERENTLY

In listening to other men who had gone through the loss of their wives, I realized that people go through the grieving process differently. I even saw this in myself. I discovered there were differences in how I worked through my mourning time after Ruth died in contrast to the way I experienced grief after Judith died. As I reviewed what was different and why, it became apparent that many factors were not the same: I was older, I no longer had kids at home, I had done it before, and I talked to more people about it the second time. Many things can affect how a person goes through the grieving process. A few include:

- The personality type of the person mourning
- The definition of the relationship between the bereaved and the loss/person lost
- The way the loss took place, whether over time or suddenly
- The coping skills of the griever and the stability of their mental health
- The support team available
- The culture and religious perspective of the one who experienced loss
- The social and financial situation they are in, or come into, based on the loss
- The age of the grieving person

A PROCESS NOT AN EVENT

Another important realization for me was to accept that grieving is a process and not an event. My personality wanted to experience it as an event, fix it and get on with life. Not so! As waves of emotion continued to well up month after month, I realized that, little by little, I was letting go of my losses with each "first" life event after my wife's death. The first holiday, the first time her birthday came up, the first time seeing mutual friends without her, and the first wedding anniversary. These were all events in the process that required time to happen and heal.

Beware of implying that a mourner should "snap out of it" too quickly. "This is behind you now," and "It's time to get on with your life," are both comments that imply just that. Prematurely stated comments to that effect can do more harm than good. Listening closely to the bereaved within the first year of a loss can reveal what comments will help them most. Beware of making comments that begin with "you should" or even "you will." Better would be statements like, "I'm not sure what to say, but I want you to know I care."

I experienced the re-establishment of a new identity after the loss of my job and position. I had to rebuild a new set of friends and lifestyle after we moved across country as a family. It is all a process and not an event.

A NATURAL EMOTIONAL RESPONSE

I came to see grief as an emotional condition that's as natural as bleeding when my arm gets cut. As a man, that was hard to acknowledge at first. I remember thinking when I was younger that if my wife's parents died, she would really cry a lot. I refused to think my emotions would be "reduced" to sobbing.

But the moment I watched Ruth take her last breath, I was suddenly overwhelmed with an emotion I didn't know was possible. It completely controlled me for a time. My heart was broken and it was as real as any other human hurt.

Mental logic such as, "Look what you have to be thankful for," or "She is in a better place" did nothing for my hurting heart. I found more solace in comments like, "I really miss her too."

FEELING OF HOPELESSNESS

Hopelessness is a word that accurately describes the hurt of the grieving. The inability to reverse the loss can be devastating. I could not bring my wife back from the dead. I could not get my position and job back. I could not recover the money I lost in a business deal. I could not bring my friends back into my life after they moved away. Things were out of control and it was scary.

Knowing what to say when helping the bereaved with the sense of hopelessness depends on the circumstances and timing. In many cases reassurances that times will be better in the future and that this hardship will pass are in order. Other times the best thing to say would be, "It must really hurt for you to be going through this now."

Comments that minimize or gloss over the loss are of little help to the griever, especially near the time of the loss. "Things will be better," "You can always have another child," "You'll get another job," or "You will find another wife" are comments that do nothing to relieve the broken heart. A simple, "I'm sorry for your loss" is better than attempting to predict the future.

GRIEF IS ABOUT THE GRIEVER

The grieving process is about the **pain of the griever** and **not the one lost**. Try to identify with the hurt the mourner is going through instead of logically dealing with the one (or thing) lost. No one really knows how any other person feels or what it is like for them. We can be the most help by focusing on helping them identify and often express their feelings with the goal of healing and victory.

A comment that can actually enrage a mourner is "I know how you must feel." WRONG. Even if you have experienced a similar loss, you really don't know exactly how someone else is feeling. There will be unknown variables that can affect the way loss grips another person. Beware of comparisons in an effort to minimize their pain. Acknowledgement of their pain is more helpful than trying to redefine yours.

IT TAKES TIME

Grieving takes time to process. Both the bereaved and those who help them must allow for the time factor. However, the amount of time required varies greatly from person to person. Many people advised me to not make any major decisions for 12 months. That may be a generalized statement, but it can be very inappropriate to demand of all grievers. Some people intently work through their grieving process in months where others require years. When seeking to aid someone who has experienced a loss, beware of predetermining a time frame for them.

Instead of saying, "So, are you doing better now?" or "You look like you are on the mend," ask your mourning friend, "How is today going for you?" This will give more room for the ups and downs of the process without making them feel wrong if they are having a bad day.

True, time does heal the mourner. When processed well, grieving does come to a conclusion. There can be a certain amount of comfort from knowing that the hurt felt today will not be forever. It is also true that time does not completely erase memories or even a bit of sadness.

That truth was shared with me from a total stranger a few weeks after Ruth's death. The shop keeper/owner was obviously approaching retirement. His friendly demeanor made it easy to share my recent experience of loss. Upon hearing my story he simply stared out the window and recalled his wife's death ten years before. "Yes," he continued, "you never really get over the loss. It is just that the pain and difficult memories fade in time."

It is interesting to note that the Bible even connects mourning with time. "To everything there is a season and a time to every purpose under heaven. ... A time to weep, and a time to laugh; a time to mourn, and a time to dance." New King James Version, Ecclesiastes 3.1, 4.

ACTION REQUIRED

Time alone is not enough to process one's pain. Some steps, however, cannot be totally ignored forever. Actions are required to victoriously emerge one day from the pit of despair. Not processing grief well is like sneezing while holding your nose and shutting your mouth. You can blow something else out!

One action step I struggled with concerned experiencing all the "firsts" that followed my wife's death. These included the first time seeing friends since my loss, the firsts of each major holiday, the first spring day, the first social event, the first time going to familiar places, the first anniversary of my loss, and even the first time having a meal with my family after my wife's funeral. Being able to experience a one-year cycle of life, and going through all the "firsts," could possibly be one of the reasons that twelve months is generally promoted in the grieving process.

I also had to process the scope of my loss. For many, coming to grips with the permanence of their loss becomes one of the hardest actions. Life as one knows it has stopped. Resulting changes required by one's loss, such as help with household chores, companionship, intimacy, help with decisions, can take time and struggle. Identifying these losses and the required changes is where long conversations can aid in the dissecting of the details of one's loss. Consequently, grief can actually be layered and needs to be peeled back like an onion.

Often, identifying with the struggles of the bereaved can only be acquired by being with them. "Call me if there is anything I can do," only confuses the mourner. They will never call you. First, they could feel "weak" if they admitted need. Second, they often aren't thinking as clearly as usual, making a simple call to a friend for help an impossibility. I suggest you show up at their place (or make a phone call) and say, "I've been thinking about you and just felt I should come by."

With the loss of my wife, I needed to realize that I lost more than just a family member. I lost my lover. I lost my best friend. I lost all the dreams for the future we had. I lost my connection to certain friends. I lost a relationship of intimacy. Each of these losses required adjustment by me. I felt like someone had torn apart my Lincoln Log house I had built over the years and I now needed to rebuild it. But many of the core pieces were missing.

DOING LIFE AGAIN

The days immediately following a loss can be a blur or even a fog, but life goes on. A friend, Michael, described it this way. "So how do you live, how do you survive? You focus on the "have-tos" first. I have to work. I have to shower. I have to eat. I have to keep up the house. I have to take care of the others in the household that are hurting just as much or more than I am. I have to hold them, comfort them. Focus on helping them get through this, while dealing with the reality that such a big part of our lives has been torn from us. That's all there is for a while. Down times are the worst. Grief, mourning, pain, tears come. My pain, pain to my kids, pain to everyone who feels the loss seems overwhelming. Focus on things that matter; things that make a difference. Songs on the radio that you sang together bring tears again. Life will never be the same!"

GRIEF AND IDENTITY

People respond differently by suddenly having the stigma or identity of being the one who has experienced a loss. Taking on the title of widow vs. married, unemployed vs. having a job, homeless vs. having a secure abode, single again vs. married, or even childless vs. cuddling a baby becomes a struggle in and of itself. This new identity is required to fully find release from the pain of the event. It can be part of the process to freedom.

The pastor of the church we were attending was a great counselor for me during Ruth's seven-year illness and death. I would often go and just tell him everything that was going on. One time, just before she died, I was in his office reviewing the events of the week. The doctors had sent her home from the hospital to die. He sensed that I was about to explode but could not. He wisely and lovingly said, "David, Ruth is dying." His stating that stark and awful truth released my emotions. I found that acknowledgement necessary to help me process my loss after she died.

Accepting the new identity that loss demands, however, needs to be processed well. I recall observing my mother's response to being "the poor widow" with five kids. She actually got to where she enjoyed the pity that identity offered. She actually became good at reminding people that she was widowed so they would possibly pity her. This became a hindrance to her healing.

In contrast, I recall the day about three months after Judith died when I sensed I was beginning to accept my singleness. It seems that from the time of Judith's funeral till that day, I could not be content to let a conversation rest with someone who did not know me until I made them aware of the fact that I was recently widowed. The identity of being a recent widower held me captive. Then, one evening, I was at a concert and struck up a conversation with the gentleman sitting beside me. When I got home I realized that I did not even mention anything about my being a recent widower. I was simply me, a single man. It felt freeing.

A person is now faced with the challenge of building a new identity, starting over. This can be scary. It requires effort. Who they are now, after their loss, needs to be redefined. This can include things like making new friends, adjusting their social calendar, maybe visiting places and people they have not seen before, and it may even mean changes in wardrobe or decorating that reflect them now. Often, part of the struggle is getting past the question, "Would my loved one approve?" or "Am I being disloyal to them by changing?"

As the griever passes through this part of the process, you can help them by changing the nature of your questions. Instead of asking how they are doing with the loss of their loved one, begin asking specific questions about them. Of course, talking about their loved one is always in order for their healing. Eventually asking specific questions about them will be helpful as they establish a new identity. "What kind of music do you like these days?" or "Would you like to go out with some friends this Friday?" can be starters. One couple at my church asked me regularly what movies I was enjoying lately. It helped that they were asking about ME and who I was now.

GRIEF HURTS

This may seem like it should go without saying: Grief hurts. However, I didn't really know to what extent it hurts until I experienced it firsthand. The pain of the mourner comes from deep inside them. It cannot be fixed quickly, nor should we think they "aren't doing well" when this pain shows up.

Six months after Judith died, I was invited to have lunch with a hospice chaplain who himself had lost his wife about the same time as me. Someone who knew me and saw me weekly had told him I needed to talk because I wasn't "handling things well." At the end of the two-hour meal, the chaplain leaned back in his seat and admitted, "I asked to meet with you today because I heard you weren't doing well. The truth is you have helped me beyond belief. Thanks."

It made me wonder why this other friend who saw me more often thought I wasn't handling things well. As I reviewed our visits, I realized what had happened. The friend who saw me weekly witnessed me tearing over easily and regularly in public. He concluded, albeit inaccurately that it must mean I was not doing well. In reality, because I had the freedom to show, my occasional painful moments, I was actually doing great in terms of working through the process.

Another important thing in understanding grief and pain is the truth in the statement that "hurting people hurt people."

As you strive to help those you know who grieve, please give room for them to express themselves. Sometimes in fits of pain they can hurt others. This may not even be intentional. An understanding heart and a polite, timely word would be much better than judgment, criticism or pulling away from them.

NOT A QUICK FIX

The list of helpful and not so helpful comments I heard during the viewing and funerals of both my wives is confusing. Many came from an effort to "fix" or help relieve my grief. If someone does not feel they have such a statement they feel like they "don't know what to say." Grief does not have a "quick fix." Grief only needs to be heard and identified, in most cases. Listening is better than talking. Statements of the loss are better than logic for why or results of the loss.

NO PRESCRIBED LIST

My personality likes predictability and lists. It frustrated me when I heard others describe their journey and I noted differences. I wondered if it was just me or them that was missing something. I finally came to the realization that although grief patterns exist, there is no such thing as a definite checklist of things every mourner must go through to process their loss well.

This helps explain why some people would question whether I was really doing well if I had not experienced a certain thing (i.e. anger, guilt, blame, "WHY?", etc.). Knowing possible feelings like this can be helpful to identify what a person is going through and accept it. However, to use any set of expectations as a checklist, much less judge a person on how well he or she is doing, can put undue stress on your relationship by adding wrong expectations.

ONE'S FAITH CAN BE CHALLENGED

I was recently interviewed over the Internet for an online TV talk show. During the interview a viewer texted in, "How did you handle your "Why God?" question?" I realize that often times this is one of the first questions grievers ask. My answer was not as some would have expected. (See the complete response in chapter 12).

One's worldview, especially regarding the spiritual side of man, tends to emerge during times of loss due to death. The "why" questions bring out fundamental beliefs, or the lack thereof, regarding basic human experiences from "origin" to "purpose" to "conclusions" surrounding human existence. Grievers often express their questions amidst their hurts. This topic can be a source of comfort for many but a source of distress for others. Your sensitivity to the griever in this area is crucial in helping process and move on to victory.

◆

« Point To Ponder »

Grief is the acknowledgement of loss emotionally. It is mostly a heart problem, not a mind challenge.

WHAT TO SAY

WHAT NOT TO SAY

- ✓ **It's so good you have the freedom to cry/express your feelings.**

    - ✗ *You need to get over this.*

- ✓ **No, you are not crazy. You are grieving and it is okay. This will pass.**

    - ✗ *I know EXACTLY how you feel.*

- ✓ **I realize this must be hard for you.**

    - ✗ *Call if you ever need anything.*

- ✓ **So, how are you feeling today?**

    - ✗ *Let me tell you what you need to do.*

- ✓ **I understand that you feel the way you do...and it is okay.**

    - ✗ *You can't bring him/her back.*
      God is in control.

"While grief is fresh, every attempt to divert only irritates. You must wait till it be digested, and then amusement will dissipate the remains of it."

SAMUEL JOHNSON

Chapter 3

—

WHEN DEATH STOLE MY WIFE – TWICE

My personal experience of losing two spouses

In addition to the simple loss of a member of the family, when a spouse dies a love relationship is lost. This can be a bigger hurdle to overcome than the simple tragic loss of a life. For me, this part of loss took me to a deeper level of hurt than simply missing someone I loved.

"He (she) was the love of your life. You must really ache now," is a better statement than, "You must move on now." Having a friend or relative acknowledge the love lost aspect helps the griever feel understood.

LOVE ESTABLISHED

"Till death do us part…" I repeated. Those words seemed to echo throughout the huge college chapel following my promise and then my bride's commitment. The witnesses of our wedding stood by smiling. Our parents sat with proud looks on their faces. In all honesty, however, I only viewed those words as a symbol of commitment. I did not really think I would experience that part of those important words, let alone do it twice.

Ruth and I had never been happier than we were that delightful day in July. The few people gathered were the family and friends who could travel to the school in the Midwest for this important event. We purposely chose the campus chapel because it "required" both sides of the family to travel and did not favor one over the other with the convenience of not having to travel. We actually were so much in love and committed to each other that we didn't care who else was there besides us.

LOVE DEVELOPED

Our relationship had developed deeply over the previous four years. We met at a large student conference our freshman year of college. The challenge, however, came from developing our relationship over the miles. I was at a school in Kansas City, Missouri, while Ruth was in nursing school in Washington, DC. Nonetheless, that challenge became a source of strength for our relationship.

The first three years of our getting acquainted happened through writing letters and occasional long distance phone calls. I say this strengthened our relationship because it forced both of us to express our hearts, feelings and beliefs on paper without the distraction of the physical arena. I recall many times when I actually had to "find" something to write to her about. That was a great boost for my growth toward her both emotionally and mentally. My heart nearly burst the glad day when Ruth said "Yes!" to me and moved to the same school I was attending for the year of our engagement. Our wedding became the highlight of our lives to that point.

Once married, to keep our growth together on a "roll" we spent every one of our wedding anniversaries – alone – discussing the "state of our union."

LOVE AT RISK

But the day came when I dreaded that event. It was the summer following Ruth's cancer diagnosis, surgeries, chemotherapy and our loss of "normal." Those events proved to be the biggest challenge to our relationship to date. Up to this point our love had been a mutual give and receive. Now Ruth was so drained physically and emotionally that she literally had nothing left to give — either to me or our four young children

As usual, however, I heeled in and took over all her household chores, protected her from the outside world and did my teaching and administration duties at the college as well. So, that went well for a few weeks, till I began to wear down emotionally and physically as well. Finally, for the first time, I sensed our relationship changing. That realization hurt. Ruth was no longer able to contribute to our relationship as before. And, in brutal honesty, I found myself questioning my love for her — simply because things seemed to be one-sided for the first time.

GUILT OVERWHELMED

Guilt was another factor added to my mourning the loss of normal life. Most likely it was because I found myself acting on Ruth's behalf out of duty and not out of emotion. I kept giving to her physically and emotionally even though she could not give back like before. I was in pain.

During those difficult days, I remember thinking to myself *if one more person asks me how my wife is doing with no obvious concern for me, someone is going to get slapped.* Finally, one close friend drove a long distance to come see me. When he arrived, I began giving him the usual update on Ruth and he stopped me. "I came to see how YOU are doing. I know Ruth is getting good care. What about you?" he replied.

I wept.

Things began to look a bit brighter after that for both of us. Ruth recovered from the effects of treatments and my spirit found strength from God. However, I began dreading our anniversary in July. How will she take hearing me admit to her that I had doubted my love for her? Would she pull back and be depressed?

That dreaded day came for our annual "state of our union"

discussion, and sure enough, Ruth asked how I had been during the throes of the hardest days that winter. I hesitantly shared with her openly how I had struggled and how God met me. She simply said, "I thought so. It's okay."

The following six years we were on an emotional roller coaster of hope and disappointment. We faced treatments and then recurrences, over and over.

A close friend at the school I taught at "held Ruth's hand" through those ups and downs. She could tell by my countenance many days how Ruth was doing. If I looked "down," Lucille would make her way to Ruth's bedroom for a chat and a prayer. Often she just sat and listened. Many times there was really nothing anyone could say, but just having someone acknowledge our pain was enough.

Wonderfully, our last year together had several highlights. We had the joy of going on a cruise. But, the most memorable time happened during our "state of our union" talk on a hot July day on the eastern shore of Lake Michigan. We sat talking and during a warm embrace Ruth softly said, "I have never felt so at one with you."

LOVE LOST

Three short months later, I watched her take her last breath. I didn't know a human could hurt so much. Within days I became aware of this hole in my soul that seemed permanent.

Friends that would cry in my presence helped more than they knew. I was still struggling a bit about embracing the grieving process, thinking it a weakness. People who cried with me gave me freedom to mourn. Positive comments about Ruth's life were also encouraging.

Most people simply said, "I am so sorry." That did help.

The grieving process was really foreign to me. I quickly learned that in much of the mourning I had no control, let alone actually causing it by some sort of weakness. That was freeing to understand. Some of my attention was diverted from my needs in order to help others deal with her death. All around me were the kids, her parents, many close friends and church folks going through various levels of grieving her loss — mother, daughter, friend. But I alone was her spouse.

WHAT TO SAY

I remember a few of the feeble comments different folks shared with me. The ones I remember most were the simple, honest statements about my present pain or loss. "I really miss her, too," one friend expressed. That empathy hugged my soul. Another had three Bible verses and a mini-sermon on God's will for me. I cringed during their comments. Being sensitive to the current need of the grieving takes care and discernment. Often their need revolves simply around their human pain at the moment. Simply stating or allowing them to state the obvious can release some of that pain.

A comment that was particularly disconcerting to me was from a well-meaning friend who told me that, "If you had had more faith, Ruth would not have had to die." Others were nearly as hurtful — the ones who AVOIDED me. I felt rejected by them. It would have been better to send a card or simply say, "I am sorry for your loss," than to say nothing and stay away.

THE LONELINESS

The next blow in the grieving process came at about three weeks. I began to realize that people were slowly pulling away from me. I felt like I was just getting into the grieving process while everyone else was "getting on" with their lives without her. Loneliness began to creep into my being. I had never experienced such inner devastation before. Many admitted to me later that they did not know what to say, so they did nothing and pulled back. It would have been a big help to me for someone to meet with me, without me asking. It would have helped so much just to be able to verbally review my journey without a long list of logical response statements offered to try and erase my pain. Just listening aids in the release process.

SEX AND GRIEVING

A few close friends have asked me how it was sexually to lose my wife. At the risk of being misunderstood, I will say a bit about that. I have bounced this off other people who have lost a spouse and not all have had this experience, but many did. One month after Ruth's funeral I began to "burn" sexually. I struggled in my mind and body sexually. This lasted about three weeks. I endured through it with prayer, activity, cold showers and long walks. I certainly was too ashamed to talk to anyone about this. So I endured till it faded. One thing that confused me was that I never sensed any guilt for my struggles. I simply took note and went on.

LEAN INTO MOURNING

It was my privilege to find a mentor in a leader from another school who had gone through the same loss of his wife while in leadership. His counsel wisely encouraged me to embrace my grief and experience it fully to ensure wholeness later on. Amidst my confusion about what he meant. I did that.

However, the silence of my friends still haunted me. So, I sought out other people who had lost a spouse to talk with. I needed to talk through my whole experience to gain perspective and relief. I am grateful to those friends who may not have known how to help me personally, but referred me to others who could identify through their own experience.

NEED TO TALK

The sixth month after Ruth's death held me hostage to my pent-up pain. I had to talk to someone. That is when I called others who had lost a mate and asked if we could talk. It turns out that I needed several two-hour conversations instead of an occasional five-minute "How are you doing?" talks. Over the next two months I found five people who understood.

Love songs and even emotional, patriotic songs, seemed to trigger my heart-sense of loss. I had never had my heart broken in a love-lost relationship before. Some days it absorbed my being. It would have helped to have someone help me identify or at least empathize with me about that part of my loss. There were some really bad days as I hurt over the "broken" relationship with Ruth.

CLOSURE

Late that spring, the "guilt" within me swelled out of control. I had to do something. So, I got in my van and drove to the graveyard where Ruth was buried. I looked to heaven and said. "Jesus, I can't talk to Ruth but YOU can. Would You tell her I am sorry?" I dropped to my knees and sobbed uncontrollably. My guilt wasn't over anything I had done that I needed to admit. It was simply how the pain of the loss of our relationship emerged. That event became a line in the sand for the conclusion of my mourning process.

In time, I began to no longer feel as if everyone was looking at me because I was alone. Working through the aspects of grief brought a new sense of wholeness to me. I began to sense stability in my emotions. The private sobbing sessions were fewer and fewer.

LOVING AGAIN

Later that year, a widow lady came to the school where I taught who absolutely swept me off my feet. I mean, I don't know what I thought about "love at first sight" before that, but the fact that it happened to me was for sure. I thought all those feelings had died. What a beautiful lady!

The next year Judith and I found ourselves in a large church in Edmonton, Alberta, Canada, with six sons on one side and two daughters and Judith's sister on the other. Again, the room echoed our vows, "Till death do us part."

These words had much deeper meaning to both of us. We had both experienced this hard reality of that truth to the fullest. However, even with that, we viewed the actuality of it happening again as being a life-time away.

Falling in love again was fun. There, I said it. A lot of the unknowns about life and love had been answered for both of us. All we needed to do was plug each other into the equation. Of course, we had to establish a new identity between us. Our new identity was a new "US." It was not like our parents' relationship. It was not like our previous marriage relationships. It was a unique, new relationship that required learning and growing together. So, we did that.

LIFE CHALLENGES LOVE

Difficult days can either make you bitter or better. Judith and I clung to each other and chose the latter. Growth and mistakes of our kids only drove us to each other. We learned early on to talk about everything, no matter how hard the subject.

I know that one of the reasons for our long-term success in blending families revolved around the tightness of Judith's and my relationship. The kids saw that we were solid and nothing they could say or do would divide us. At the end of each day, no matter how difficult the issues of the day, Judith and I were in each other's arms.

About 15 years after we said "I do," Judith's health began to be of concern. She seemed to lose energy early in the day. At the time my job included a lot of travel. I began to see that she could no longer take as many trips as we had in previous years. The ensuing five years involved chasing symptoms from doctor to doctor. Each doctor only dealt with the symptoms she described and not one could connect them to a cause. We both knew something was seriously wrong, but were helpless about what to do since there was no definitive diagnosis. We faced her health issue together. We intentionally worked hard on her health, even though we did not know what we were fighting.

While visiting family, Judith suddenly had symptoms resembling a stroke. An MRI revealed a mass on her brain. We were told it had to come out. During that surgery, the doctor called me in the waiting room. He said, "Mr. Knapp, I am sorry. I am seldom surprised but much to my surprise, I found a very mean looking cancer tumor on Judith's brain that came from somewhere else." I immediately knew she was going to die. I sat down and sobbed uncontrollably for nearly an hour. My sobbing continued daily from that day in August until Christmas day.

DEATH CHALLENGES LOVE

The next day a full-body scan exposed cancerous spots on her lungs and a large, stage four tumor on her pancreas. With that news Judith asked, "Does that mean I am going to die?" I teared up and nodded, "Yes" as I leaned over for a long, sobbing embrace. I had never heard Judith cry like that before.

Just as Judith and I talked about everything, this would be no different. The next four days in the hospital afforded us time to mourn her impending death together. Few visitors were allowed in. It was our time to fully say goodbye and discuss the possible events of the coming months. As usual, we tackled even the hard questions. Through our tears we discussed issues like helping the kids and grandkids through the mourning process, what her memorial service would look like, would she want to die at home with hospice, and her even insisting that I, again, consider remarriage.

FACING DEATH

The pain and release of talking about her death with Judith was a new event for me. Ruth and I never did that. I guess it was because we were so young and clung to all hope for even a few more months together that we avoided actually looking at each other and admitting out loud that she was going to die now.

Gradually we communicated with our eight children and their families that they needed to do whatever it took to come see Mom/Grandma soon before pain medication made it hard for her to be alert. Consequently, over the following six weeks, each of our kids, their spouses and the twenty-four grandkids came one family at a time. Each had one-to-one personal time with Judith saying goodbye and expressing abiding love that only she could give. It was the most heart-wrenching thing I have ever had to do for such a long time. I watched, monitored and participated in each one's mourning. Some of the grandchildren wept the deepest in my arms.

TALK ABOUT DEATH

We did have hospice come oversee Judith's care. However, I cared for her myself at nights, till the last four weeks. A long-time friend helped a few days during the day and then Judith's sister and one of our daughters were able to come help me for those final weeks. This meant that her sister would sleep with Judith at night so I could get better rest. That seemed to work for a couple weeks. However, about two weeks before she left us, Marsha told me that she thought Judith was needing me more because she was really restless at night. So, I started "putting her to bed" after her physical needs were met. Everyone would leave and I would kneel down beside her head. I talked to her, prayed with her and rubbed her arms. This worked well, as she began resting better after that.

About a week before she left for heaven, I was talking to her quietly at her bedside and a tear trickled down the side of her face. Through her medicated fog she whispered, "I'm sorry I have to die." Now I was having tears running down my cheek. I assured her it was okay and that I would be fine. I gave her permission to go on without me and that I would be along soon.

On an early Sunday morning late in October, Judith leaped into the arms of Jesus. She was free from the pain. My mourning plunged to the deepest level I had ever experienced. I felt like I was a no-body with her gone.

My grief was inconsolable. Marsha and Kathy, wisely, simply hugged me and proceeded to take care of physical needs in the house.

GRIEVING NOT EASY

Several people since have asked me if it was easier or harder to mourn the loss of a spouse the second time. My response is that it was harder for me. I cite two reasons for this conclusion. The first time the mourning process was new to me and each stage was a bit of a surprise. This time, I knew how much I would have to hurt before I could heal. That was hard. My relationship with Ruth was "text-book" in many ways. Our marriage had developed well from our youth to age 41. However, neither one of us had really experienced deep hurt.

Judith and I entered our marriage having both experienced the deep pain of grieving well. This made it possible for us to love deeply which becomes my second reason. My emotional loss was deeper due to this deeper level of love Judith and I enjoyed and pursued.

DEALING WITH LONELINESS

I was alone again. This time was different. The first time I had an empty bed but a house full of kids to keep caring for. This time, I came home to an empty bed and an empty house. The loneliness was deafening.

A few friends offered in passing, "Dave, if you ever want to talk, call me anytime. I mean it, anytime." Well guess what? It didn't happen. I knew they had lives and families. I probably could have called. I probably should have called. But it would have been more helpful if they had said, "So, Dave, would it be better if I came by Saturday at 7 p.m. or Sunday?"

I knew from previous experience to expect my friends to begin to pull away after about three weeks. They did. It did not hit me with surprise because I understood more this time. So, like before, I intentionally did things to allow the grieving process to happen instead of hiding or stuffing it. I would plan to go out in the evenings, even if it meant going to the mall and watching people go by while eating an ice cream cone or going to a movie … alone.

EXPERIENCING THE "FIRSTS"

A common counsel often given to grievers is to not make any major decisions for the first 12 months. I began to think this through as to *why one year?* I realized soon that twelve months gives time for a normal cycle of life and the opportunity to go through most of the "firsts" after the loss. These events include: First birthdays, First holiday seasons, First time talking to friends and relatives, First season changes, First time in familiar settings, etc. So, I realized I can "lean into" the process by doing these "Firsts" intentionally.

It was my blessing to have friends and family who understood that. They were very cooperative when I connected with them about visits and going out to social events with them.

SEX & GRIEVING AGAIN

One month after Judith's body was taken away it happened again. I began to struggle sexually again. At least it was not such a surprise. I noticed again that my struggles did not include guilt. I wanted to understand what was going on — and continue to deal with the struggle successfully. I had been open with Judith about this happening to me after Ruth's death. She surprised me to say it happened to her as well. She felt bad about it.

Finally, in the middle of the night I put some things together. In the past I have helped several men deal with the addiction to pornography. In my researching how to help them I learned that science has identified that sexual enjoyment comes from the same part of the brain as other addictions that we consider hardcore. I began to realize that it is a very real possibility that our healthy sex life was like an addiction to my brain and that when it was totally gone (not even able to touch her hand) within thirty days I went through a "dry out" time. This time was physical and not moral, hence no need for guilt. I am not a professional in all this by education. But, the concept has helped me and others with whom I have shared it.

The hormones that are released during sex have been identified. The *CharismaNews* blog, May 13, 2015, contained an article by Tiana & Jeremy Wiles entitled "Sex Before Marriage Rewires Your Brain" that explains the sexual brain. Oxytocin is a hormone produced primarily in women's bodies. This is released during sex and makes her bond with her husband emotionally. Men produce vasopressin, which is also referred to as the "monogamy hormone." The release of vasopressin bonds a man emotionally to his wife. When death of a spouse occurs, it is possible to go into withdrawals when the body and brain is deprived of these hormones.

SOCIAL FIRSTS

Many of the firsts came by surprise. The first time I was out socially with people who did not know me I was blindsided with the question, "So where is your wife?" I startled everyone with my reply of, "She is in heaven." Silence. I knew I was progressing the first time I was in a similar situation and I did not feel like the conversation was complete until everyone knew I was recently widowed. I was beginning to develop a new identity without Judith.

Although no one emerged to review the various stages of my grieving process, I realized from experience the value of addressing this. So, I would send a "How Dad's Doing" email to my adult children periodically, reviewing points of progress and transition in my grieving process. That was a help to me as well as to them.

SINGLE AGAIN

One reality of being widowed was the challenge of thinking of myself as a whole single person and not a half of a couple. My friends struggled with that as well. Some struggled with it so much that they have pulled away from me. And for some, in a subtle way, they viewed me as a threat when it came to their wives. It sounds strange, but it is often true for both widowers and widows in social settings. Somehow being single is often associated with being promiscuous in some way, or at the very least "available."

LOSS IS COMMON

Finally, don't be afraid to educate yourself about the grieving process. Most people mistakenly think the mourning process is purely an emotional condition, ignoring that it is a physical condition as well. If you are married, it WILL happen to one of you, eventually. My case is unusual only because it happened during younger years. Dying happens among the elderly every day.

« Point to Ponder »

Mourners are sensitive to unsupportive comments that seem to minimize their grief.

WHAT TO SAY

WHAT NOT TO SAY

- ✓ **Can I help you find others who have had a similar loss?**

    - ✗ *This happened because God had something/someone better for you.*

- ✓ **Can you join our group for dinner this Friday?**

    - ✗ *Call me sometime.*

- ✓ **His/her memories are a legacy of love.**

    - ✗ *You need to let go of him/her so you can start living again.*

- ✓ **Are you up for a chat now or next week?**

    - ✗ *You look great. You must be over it.*

- ✓ **Thanks for having the freedom to talk to me about your feelings right now.**

    - ✗ *How are you holding up?*

"But there is a discomfort that surrounds grief. It makes even the most well-intentioned people unsure of what to say. And, so many of the freshly bereaved end up feeling even more alone."

MEGHAN O'ROURKE

Chapter 4

—

WHEN DEATH STEALS A SPOUSE

Special help when aiding those who lost a spouse through death

I attended a stress management seminar in Detroit many years ago. During that seminar I learned that on a national average the top two highest stress-producing events were public speaking and the death of a spouse. During the months following Ruth's death my reading included information on dealing with the loss of a spouse. Among the statements about the importance of taking care of your own health while you grieved, the point emerged that among older people the possibility of the surviving spouse dying often increased by forty percent in the year following the loss. It is not necessary for anyone to be a statistic in the national averages. These facts do, however, emphasize the significance of losing a beloved spouse.

TO BE RECKONED WITH

The doorway to my bedroom seemed to jerk me to a sudden stop. Staring at the spot where I watched my wife take her last breath three weeks earlier, I melted into another uncontrolled sobbing session. My daily wandering around the house like a two-year-old child looking for a pacifier seemed endless.

This time I ended the emotional session by thinking of other deep hurts I had experienced. I perceived them differently now. My mom came to mind. Suddenly my situation seemed not so harsh. *Wow*, I thought, *She really had life tough when my dad died suddenly!* For my whole life I only could remember the difficult years surrounding my dad's accident from my 11-year-old boy's perspective. But now, through my own loss, my heart ached for my mom and I admired her in new ways.

I was the oldest of four kids the day of my dad's accident. Mom was a young 30-year-old pregnant woman living in a home with no indoor plumbing and a pot belly stove that burned coal or wood for heat. Winter had only delivered half her force when our lives changed forever that sunny February day. My mother's grief seemed to cause our lives to stop. She spent a lot of time in bed and only got up to give the minimum care for her four small children. One week after my dad's funeral she delivered my youngest brother.

A week after Mom came home from the hospital with my baby brother, we got an unexpected visit from her dominating mother. She burst into our house unannounced. Upon her arrival, she found the house in a chaotic mess. Mother was in bed, as usual. It had been nearly a month since my dad was killed in the accident. The newborn at her side received all her attention at the expense of taking care of the house and the rest of us children. In retrospect, Mom's behavior was understandable given all these circumstances. Unfortunately, Grandmother responded in a very harsh fashion.

"Get out of that bed and stop this right now," my grandmother snapped. My mom had never crossed her commanding mother her entire life and she didn't start then. She did what she was told physically, but she could not deal with her grief so easily. So, instead of going through the grieving process in a healthy way, Mom stuffed it down for the present but her grief didn't stay down. The pain seeped out the rest of her life.

Difficult days for my mom continued that first year. With no husband, Mom still had a farm to manage. She had no clue how to do that and care for five kids. That spring and summer the neighbors came in force to help plant and then harvest a crop. However, she lost the farm and we had to move into the small town nearby. The only financial income Mom qualified for was government assistance. Three hundred dollars a month did not go very far, even back then. Very often, the money I got from mowing lawns supplemented to buy bread and gas.

This experience, along with the busyness of life, kept a raw place in my mother's soul. I saw her pull out Dad's picture and weep each time hard emotional events occurred. The most vivid one came during her divorce from the man she married three years after my dad's death. Her healing had been aborted and she suffered for it for years.

Sadly, my mom died relatively young of a rare disease that could have been triggered by stress. In my judgment she suffered in many ways, because her grief was not processed well.

Sometimes circumstances and dominant personalities hinder some people from grieving freely. In many of these cases, having a friend or close relative who gives them "permission" to grieve can be a key to their victory. Instead of pointing out their strength or toughness, an honest statement about their loss and pain would be more beneficial to their long-term healing. A straightforward question such as, "Are you giving yourself time or permission to cry sometimes?" could be just the thing that helps.

THE CLOSER, THE LESS

Roz called me from Florida the other day. She was hesitant but asked, "Can I ask you a question about how to help a new friend of mine?" She explained that a new lady had just started coming to her Bible study who had recently lost her husband. Roz said she wanted to help her and not be a hindrance to her. Neither of us had a long time to talk so Roz asked me for a "really concise version" of what she needed to say or not say. I replied, "The general rule is: The more recent the loss, the less you should say."

What that means is that the closer it is time-wise that the loss actually took place, the less you should say. If they lost their loved one that day, you say very little. Maybe one sentence like, "It must really hurt." Do not try to solve their mourning issue with a long logic statement on how to look ahead, etc. However, if you are talking to them three months later, you might find they want to rehearse how their loved one died in vivid detail.

Sheryl Sandberg, chief operating officer at Facebook, lost her husband in an accident. In a poignant personal post on her Facebook timeline June 3, 2015, she articulately expressed some things about her first month of grieving that demonstrate what I'm talking about with my phrase, "the closer, the less":

> I have learned that I never really knew what to say to others in need. I think I got this all wrong before; I tried to assure people that it would be okay, thinking that hope was the most comforting thing I could offer. A friend of mine with late-stage cancer told me that the worst thing people could say to him was "It is going to be okay." That voice in his head would scream, How do you know it is going to be okay? Do you not understand that I might die? I learned this past month what he was trying to teach me. Real empathy is sometimes not insisting that it will be okay but acknowledging that it is not. When people say to me, "You and your children will find

happiness again," my heart tells me, Yes, I believe that, but I know I will never feel pure joy again. Those who have said, "You will find a new normal, but it will never be as good" comfort me more because they know and speak the truth. Even a simple "How are you?"—almost always asked with the best of intentions—is better replaced with "How are you today?" When I am asked, "How are you?" I stop myself from shouting, My husband died a month ago, how do you think I am? When I hear, "How are you today?" I realize the person knows that the best I can do right now is to get through each day."

THE ROLLER COASTER

Grieving the loss of a spouse is not an event; it is a process. This process can take one from emotional highs to deep grief without warning.

Judith stopped in her tracks and stared at the silhouette filling the doorway. Gordon (her husband) had died just weeks before. She and her sister were out shopping on a much-needed reprieve. Gordon had been six foot six inches in stature and built like "Mr. Clean." The man in the doorway grabbed her attention. "Judith," Marsha began, "Are you okay?" The swell of emotion engulfed Judith, right there in the clothing department.

Marsha's response to this normal event in the healing

process of a mourner was right on. She did not try to talk Judith down or out of the emotions that swelled up. She did not criticize her for expressing her emotions openly. Instead, she came along side and saw it as normal and healthy and just let her cry.

One of the common errors I have seen in those who are friends of the bereaved emerges when they see their friend show emotions and somehow think that it is not good, or a sign they are struggling. The common implication is that a lack of emotion signifies they are doing okay. This isn't true. Public display of emotions can be a sign that the bereaved is freely working through the process and can be very "normal."

I have received negative feedback from friends who witnessed my public expression of emotion. Some saw it as weakness, while others concluded I must not have been doing well. In fact, the opposite was true. I experienced added healing each time I had the freedom to express these sudden bouts of emotions. To deny someone this freedom of emotional expression could be a hindrance to their healing.

Author Jerry Sittser, in his book *A Grace Disguised* explains it this way:

> Giving myself to grief proved to be hard as well as necessary. It happened in both spontaneous and intentional ways. I could not always determine the proper time and setting for tears, which occasionally came at unexpected and inconvenient moments, such as in the middle of a college class I was

teaching or during a conversation. I was surprised to see how inoffensive that was to others. If anything, my display of grief invited them to mourn their own losses, and it made the expression of sorrow a normal and natural occurrence in daily life. (pg. 42)

When this happens in your presence instead of saying something to try to stop their tears it would be better to say, "It's okay. I know it must hurt sometimes more than others. I miss them too. Thanks for having the freedom to cry in front of me."

TIME WELL SPENT

Understanding the depth of emotion a friend or relative is going through can go a long way in helping you know how to assist them in their journey. Often this can only be found out by spending time with that person and listening closely. You may even need to ask clear questions. A simple, "How are you doing?" will not produce a true picture. A better question may be, "Can you tell me about your up and down feelings today (or this week)?"

A friend of mine who lost his wife eight months ago wrote this to me. "I believe I am doing 'well' which might need some explaining. I still get blindsided by my emotions and, for what seems like no reason at all, I have a meltdown. The pain doesn't seem as sharp and overwhelming as it has in the past, but it is there. Loneliness is hard to handle. A busy schedule helps, but a busy schedule doesn't satisfy the need to talk and interact with a person of confidence. God knows these things and I am learning how to handle the different situations that come into my life."

A listening ear and the right questions can provide needed information to you as you seek to be the best comforter to a friend or relative. Avoid statements of command that tell them to "Suck it up" or "Be strong." Those only imply that stuffing their grief is the best, when that is not the case.

WHAT IT IS ABOUT

I have noticed that, many times, the attention in loss tends to be directed towards the loved one lost. However, I'd like to suggest that one truly understands the depths of grief when it is realized that grieving needs to center around the pain of the griever.

"Your loved one has no more pain," announced the attending doctor. This response to the death of a loved one is very kind when announcing their death. The blow of the news concerning immediate loss can even be softened more with consolation that the one who has died is better off in some way. However, as time passes, the pain that the griever is experiencing overshadows any trite consolation pertaining to the deceased. Their soul is hurting beyond belief. I remember feeling like there was a hole in my soul that seemed permanent.

Statements such as, "They are in a better place," "It was their time to go," "God loved them so much He wanted them with Him in heaven," "It was God's will for them to die," or

"They are happier now" put the emphasis on the wrong place and do not benefit the griever. Grief is not a result of the change in the condition or location of the dead. It is caused by the pain being experienced by the griever because of their loss. Acknowledging and addressing the pain of the griever can be of much more help in processing them through to victory.

A NO-BRAINER

I met Bob and Rachel years ago. Bob's first wife had died suddenly a couple years before. By the time I met them, Bob and Rachel had just met. They soon married and were building a life of ministry together. Forty-one years later I got a letter from Bob saying that Rachel had died suddenly. I waited until after the three-week time frame to contact him because I knew that would be about when most people began to pull away and his need to talk would only increase.

The day we connected by phone was a Saturday morning. Some have asked me, "So, what did you say to him?" My answer is, "Very little. Mostly I just listened." About the only significant thing I said to Bob during that hour conversation was, "When I read your letter about Rachel, it broke my heart." Following his tears, he went into detail telling me everything surrounding her death. It was then I learned the startling news that Rachel had taken her life. It was obvious that he felt the need to unload the details that probably were tormenting his mind including the struggles he was having. I sensed a freedom in his spirit when he said, "Goodbye. Maybe we can talk again."

I knew that I did not *have* to know what to say to Bob; I only needed to connect with his emotional hurts and let him talk through his experiences. Grief is an emotional issue, not a brain issue. *Heart responses* help more than *logic statements* at this point.

You don't have to have a well thought out plan of logic to help the grieving. Simple concern works great.

LONELINESS

It is well worth repeating here that loneliness, to most who have lost a spouse, soon becomes a huge hurdle that can last for years.

Loneliness is a very real part of the grieving process. Loneliness can be experienced in *addition* to missing the one who has died. Thomas Wolfe puts it this way: "The whole conviction of my life now rests upon the belief that loneliness, far from being a rare and curious phenomenon, peculiar to myself and to a few other solitary men, is the central and inevitable fact of human experience."

This aspect of the grieving process is often overlooked by those not experiencing it. I found it to be suffocating. We all understand that we will miss the one whom we have lost. But, what about the oppressing loneliness that develops later? Many have expressed that, though missing their loved one was difficult, coping with the loneliness was more painful.

That being said, as you respond to those who have faced a loss, include loneliness as part of their experience in your thinking. This aspect can be easier to help them with since all of us have had bouts of loneliness in our lives. "How are you handling times of loneliness?" is a good question along with,

"When can I come by during times you are commonly feeling alone?"

YOU DON'T KNOW

"Sixty-one years is a long time to be married to the same person — and then lose them," Elaine said as she stared into space. "Wow," was my response. "That is amazing and I can't even imagine how it must feel for you now. The loneliness must be overwhelming."

"You're right, it is," was her confident reply. We went on to cover simple changes both she and I had experienced over the last year: buying food and cooking for ONE instead of two, learning to manage jobs our mates always did, and adjusting socially to being single. I noticed that her spirits and demeanor improved following our talk.

Did you notice that I did not say anything like, "I know how you feel?" or "I know, I lost two wives!" Neither statement is helpful. I really don't understand another's personal pain, and she did not expect me to. She only needed me to empathize and acknowledge her pain. And comparative statements tend to shut people down. Too often, when we don't know what to say to FIX their problem with grief, we feel we can't help and so we shy away. Not so. Grievers need to be heard, not fixed, or out-done.

EXPRESSION, NOT QUICK FIX

Expression and closure are important for those who have experienced loss.

I had the opportunity to share my experiences and lessons of going through loss at a large men's prison in southeastern California recently. The chaplain, who is a long-time friend, invited me to share with the "church" he was responsible for behind bars. It proved to be a great opportunity to offer healing.

Following my talk, men began lining up to express appreciation and tell me their stories. One impacted me in particular. A man in his early 60's with a ponytail had joined the line. When he got to me he was so emotional he couldn't talk. He stepped out of line for a moment before he composed himself enough to tell me his story. He had married his childhood sweetheart, then went to Viet Nam. He came back with severe Post-Traumatic Stress Disorder and she eventually left him. Later in life he was able to overcome the effects of the war and she returned to him. He never said why he was in prison, but while he was serving time, she died. He never got to say goodbye, nor did he have the opportunity to settle any hurts OR even go to her funeral.

My forthright talk about grief and even my facial expressions made him feel that I was the first person to come into his life who understood his pain. This rough and tough man sobbed on my shoulder for the longest time, and it gave him release.

You can be of great help to those you know by allowing them multiple opportunities to express their pain (not fix it) and thus aid them in steps of closure. It can even be helpful to ask, "Where do you see yourself in your grieving process? Tell me about it."

GET TO THE POINT

Get to the point. This is good advice for people who wish to really be of practical help to a friend or relative who has experienced a recent loss. It is very easy and tempting to make general statements like, "If there is anything I can do to help," or "Let me know what I can do."

As clear as these may seem to you it can sound more like "la la land" to the griever and require more energy than they have. Grieving takes a lot of emotional and mental energy. Often simple "yes" and "no" questions are all one can process with any level of definitiveness. Future planning skills are hampered in the minds of the bereaved. Thinking about needing groceries next week will not be a need until the minute one runs out of milk.

If you are really serious about helping your friend or relative in some physical way, specific questions are better. "Can I come over on Tuesday and help you get your housework caught up?" "I do grocery shopping on Saturday, can I call you then to see what you may need from the store?" "Is it okay if I call you Thursday evening between 8:00 and 10:00 p.m. to chat?"

IDENTITY CRISIS

Judith died early on a Sunday morning. Seeing and touching her lifeless body is permanently embedded in my memory. I walked from the bedroom to the living room and collapsed on the couch with uncontrollable sobs. I was inconsolable. As the tears lessened, my soul began to hurt and a hollow feeling overwhelmed me. I felt like a nobody. Immediately, my identity and definition of who I was vanished. I was no longer Judith's husband. She was gone. I was single again and did not know what that meant. I was no longer among the marrieds group in society. I no longer had someone to check in with concerning daily events and decisions. All future plans we had made were useless and gone!

Some have tried to explain this identity crisis caused by the loss of a spouse as an amputation of one's self. One man, following the loss of his wife, expressed it well. He likened him and his wife as a pair of pliers. With both sides present and attached, the pliers are a very useful tool. He said he felt like one side was now gone and the "pliers" could no longer grasp anything. The re-definition of one's self becomes then compounded by the difficult situation of loss due to death. It barges in as a situation that has to be worked through and not easily dealt with by immediate replacement. Some of my sense of fulfillment in life revolved around Judith's happiness and well-being. That purpose in life for me vanished.

Friends' comments that meant the most in helping me cope at this stage included, "I know how much you loved her," "I don't know how you feel right now, but I want you to know I am here for you," "I am praying for you," and "You are still very important to me."

SOCIAL ADJUSTMENTS

Being single again created many other adjustments for me. For the longest time after both of my wives' deaths I still felt married. I wore my wedding band for months after they departed. I still thought of myself as half a couple. Adjusting to my new reality and viewing myself as a whole single person took time. I began to realize that my regular circle of friends had to make the same adjustments. Some pulled away while others saw me as a threat.

Elisabeth Elliot, in her book *Loneliness* expressed it well:

> In spite of this modern shuffling of ancient norms, social gatherings are still often made up of what we (sometimes loosely) call couples. As a widow I never enjoyed being a fifth wheel. I threw things off balance simply by being there, but this was a reality I had to come to terms with. It was nobody's fault. It would be silly to protest that the married people were supposed to *do* something about my feelings in the matter. Many of them tried. Everybody was kindness itself in the beginning, hovering over me, offering helps of all sorts, inviting me out. Many continued to be kind when the so-called grieving process was supposed to be over, but there was nothing in the world they could do about my not being half of a couple anymore. (pg. 41)

HOLIDAYS CAN HURT

The first holidays after losing a spouse can be excruciating. Christmas especially looms as hard for many. Being helpful and attentive to those you know who were recently widowed can be very important.

Following Ruth's death in October, her parents were still living near us and, of course, I had four children to think about and care for. We had Thanksgiving with her parents as usual. Christmas developed differently. A good friend who lived in Grand Rapids made me an unusual offer. He had been a missionary pilot and now had his own plane. He invited us to join his family for the week of Christmas in a private cabin complex in the Bahama Islands. We only had to meet him at an airport in Florida and he would fly us over to the island and take care of us for the five days we were there. We took him up on it. The solitude was just what we needed at that time. The pain we could have experienced during the holidays was diminished.

Judith's death was also in October. I saw the month of December as an opportunity to heal through many "firsts" in my grieving process. This time I had an empty home. Two families of kids and grandkids lived nearby, but my house was empty. Early in December I flew to Iowa to attend a Christmas gathering of my many siblings and their families. I knew this would be a good opportunity to begin the Christmas season by connecting with them for the first time since Judith's death. It turned out to be a great time of healing for many of them as well as for me. I then had an evening of Christmas gifts and meals with the two families living near me. For Christmas day, however, I was alone. I thought nothing of it since I had celebrated Christmas with my kids. However, a couple hours after I got up and realized it was Christmas day, I began to sob.

I wept for several hours that morning. My healing was continuing. That afternoon I attended a community potluck meal and met some new friends that I enjoyed being with.

Both experiences, being with people in a different setting, as well as being alone helped me to reflect and heal. Some grievers continue to struggle, trying to reproduce past Christmases. Some avoid the season altogether, while others start all new traditions for the holidays. As with the grieving process itself, there is no *best* way to deal with the holidays. Dangers and benefits to each exist. It becomes important to have a plan that best suits the people involved.

You don't have to come up with an almighty solution to a griever's pain over the holidays. It is often important that you address it by asking them what their plans are for the upcoming holidays. This can give them an opportunity to talk through it and it lets them know you are aware and concerned with their pain.

WAYS TO HELP

Remember that grieving can't be "fixed." Grieving is a process to be experienced. A great way to help the mourner, can be by assisting them physically to ease life's demands while they heal.

Judith often told me about the ways many people helped her during her years of widowhood. She had four young boys and a house to maintain. Prepared food that arrived at her door became a valued treasure as she could not concentrate on preparing food and everything else. She spoke of ladies who showed up and simply came in to help clean or do dishes. Some people came to help remodel the basement in order to make it more usable. Men would take the boys and teach them to shoot or ski. Actions like this actually aided in her ability to heal. Serving becomes the same as comforting.

She pointed out that the most effective servers were people with whom she had a good relationship. Interestingly, there were those who did not make the effort to build a relationship either through service or emotionally. For them it seemed easier to do a "token task" and avoid her pain and situation altogether. But that approach to help falls short when practiced by friends.

During Judith's time of terminal illness, friends set up a website folks could go to in order to sign up to bring meals to my house. Our large circle of friends brought meals every other day for three and a half months, which made our grieving burden seem a bit lighter. Likewise, offers to come clean my house after her funeral were greatly appreciated. Though generally able to do everything before, grieving disables, if not derails, even the strongest person for a time.

TIME IS A FRIEND

To the griever who is engaged in the process TIME IS THEIR FRIEND. This can be both comforting and dreaded news. It is comforting because it assures them that time does have a healing affect in their grieving process. However, it can cause dread to those who wish grieving were a short event that is over and done in an instant and not something to experience over a length of time.

Your comments should reflect understanding that time will be an important ingredient in their grieving process. "You should put this behind you," "You should get on with your life," "Life goes on, you know," or "What's done is done" can give the wrong impression about time and grieving.

You can be more help by saying things like, "What was it like when…?" or "What are some things that have eased your pain?" or "No, you are not crazy. You are grieving." or "I remember this about your spouse…"

◆

« Point to Ponder »

Avoiding grievers socially, or avoiding the topic of their loss, stifles their grieving process.

WHAT TO SAY

WHAT NOT TO SAY

- ✓ **Here is a favorite memory I have of him/her.**
  - ✗ *So now you are all alone. What a shame.*

- ✓ **You made the right decisions surrounding his/her death.**
  - ✗ *At least he/she is not a vegetable.*

- ✓ **Can I call you on an anniversary that is important to you?**
  - ✗ *You need to get all his belongings out of the house as soon as possible.*

- ✓ **Can I come by and get your grocery list on Friday?**
  - ✗ *You are not making sense. Snap out of it.*

- ✓ **Can I come by and help clean on Tuesday?**
  - ✗ *How does it feel to have survived his/her death?*

  - ✗ *You should be thankful it wasn't worse.*

"Grief, no matter where it comes from, can only be resolved by connecting to other people."

THOMAS HORN

Chapter 5

—

WHEN LOSS STEALS A CHILD

Comforting those who have lost a child by any means

"When a child dies before the parent, the world is upside down." (Old Chinese proverb)

Ruth and I did not talk very much about her impending death those seven years she battled cancer. I am sure it would have helped us some had we done more. One of the times we did have a serious talk about her going to heaven revolved around our children. She mourned her own death often and alone. She commonly said she felt like she was being "replaced" in life. The one painful topic we talked about was her mourning her loss of our children. "I probably won't be able to see their children," she muttered through her sobs. "I'm going to miss...." She rehearsed many things about our kids that she would not be there for. I watched her affectionately rock our youngest with a faraway look in her eye. I knew she was "missing" that bond in the future and trying to enjoy it now.

This level of loss was all so new to me. I would just listen to her as she reviewed her losses. And likewise, listening is the most powerful thing a friend can do for parents who have lost a child. The hurt comes across as unusually sharp and persistent. A thoughtless comment like, "Well, it must be God's will," is not a help at all. Their pain is deeply emotional and not theological.

MAJOR STRESS

The study I referred to in chapter four on life's stress factors listed the loss of a child as being a close third behind losing a spouse and public speaking. There are factors about losing a child, however, that can be permanently stifling. No matter how many children one has (I have eight), each one is unique. There will be always enough love for each child. Each one has their own permanent place in a parent's heart. The loss of that child can never be replaced nor a substitution found. A child is irreplaceable.

I have heard well-meaning friends doing more harm than good to a grieving parent by saying thoughtless things like, "You can always have another one," "Maybe you can get a dog," and "Well at least you won't have to go through ... with this one." You will find it always much better to identify the pain of the parent with simple statements such as, "I have no idea of how much you must be hurting right now."

Recently I was privileged to meet Daniel Parkins in Southern California. Our get-acquainted conversation eventually exposed our recent losses. I was intrigued while listening to his process of dealing with his loss of a very young son to a serious illness. He lays it out well in his book about their journey entitled *Nineteen Days*:

> I'm not sure I can explain the feeling well. It's too impossibly deep for words to express. It's as many writers and poets have said throughout the centuries — the breaking of the heart in two. It's worse than anything I have felt, anything that I have heard, anything and everything cannot be compared to it — to take my son off life support, the beautiful Samuel whom we loved so desperately. Samuel, whom we prayed so fervently for and hoped for and dreamed for. Samuel, the younger brother, was now going to be missing in our lives for the rest of the sentence we were called to live. It really felt as though my son was being murdered; only I could not prevent it. I felt helpless. (pg. 144)

The Parkins were blessed with a circle of friends and colleagues who felt the pain with them and gave them lots of time and freedom to work through their grief. Their heart ached, not their long-term logic. Daniel pointed out to me that one of the very best thing received from others was that many were simply present for them and even gave silent hugs. Their loss and pain needed to be acknowledged, not explained away.

LONG-TERM COMMITMENT

The loss of a child can be one of the most difficult losses. Even the Bible sees it as a severe experience. "...make mourning, as for an only son, most bitter lamentation..." (Jeremiah 6.26b)

Helping a friend or relative grieving the loss of a child may be a long-term commitment. Unlike other losses, the loss of a child returns to the mind of the parent in a fresh way when unmet milestones come along for the life cut short. You can be most helpful by supporting these times of prolonged grief. Just remembering with the parent can help soothe a broken heart at the child's birthday or death anniversary. A card or text could go a long way to add comfort.

Loss is indeed a part of our human existence. Helping each other through these normal times increases our bonds to each other and fulfills a purpose for us being in each other's lives.

LEADERSHIP MISSED IT

A few months following Ruth's funeral, I met with a missionary couple who had been students under my teaching a few years prior. They had just returned from abroad where they served as missionaries in a remote area. While there, they had suffered the loss of a young child. During the year following that tragedy, their leadership had counseled with them that they should "get over" their loss and get on with life.

This unwise counsel only deepened their emotional pain so severely that they packed their belongings and returned home.

I listened to their story in its entirety and expressed my empathy for their grief. The few comments I made came from the depths of my own mourning experience. At one point the wife burst out, "Finally, a leader who understands! No one else has indicated an understanding ear." Her sobs flowed freely. The leadership in that area did not know what to say. Consequently, saying the wrong thing drove this dear couple away from their life's passion.

Finding oneself aiding a friend or relative who has lost a child can be a shocking place to be. Knowing what to say can be a huge help in the healing process for them. It is important to remember all the standard things about the grieving process found in chapter two. In addition to these points, a few special considerations can be beneficial both to you and to the mourner you are helping.

HUMANS HURT

It is very human for parents to hurt following the loss of a child. Emily Rapp, frequent memoir blogger and author, described her experience of losing a child:

> My son Ronan died last week before his third birthday. He'd been sick with a terminal illness for his entire life, but as a friend of mine wisely noted, 'Death and dying are very different.' Now he is dead, which has marked the beginning of a new stage of grief, one that

is characterized by deep sadness and longing, but cleaned of the mania of panic that is part of anticipatory grief.

Ronan is released from a body that could not live in this world; as his mother, I am released from watching him suffer. But we are still divided, forever and for good. I mourn him, I miss him, I'm sad. I'm angry, I'm confused, I'm scattered. I'm elated that he is free; I am ready to be happy. I'm human.

Nothing you say can make the pain go away. A caring comment cannot make it worse.

Helping to deal with the loss of a child may be a permanent part of your relationship with the bereaved parent. You can do things like sending 'thinking of you' cards on special occasions such as Mother's Day and the child's birthday. Offering to talk about the surge of feelings that can come over a grieving parent may bring tears, but remember those tears are not from hurt you created. The tears are part of the release process.

GUILT

Parents feel responsible for the welfare of their children. Parents believe they are to protect their kids from harm and even failure. In addition to the "normal" attributes of the grieving process, we need to understand the complications possible with the loss of a child. At some point, some parents need to work through guilt. The feeling that there was something they should or could have done — or not done — to prevent the death commonly emerges. This is not abnormal. Here, again, concepts from logic statements may not help the loss of the heart.

I saw this truth first-hand one evening. At the end of a concert I noticed that the mature gentleman sitting beside me wore a sweatshirt indicating he hailed from the same state I grew up in. So I asked him what part of Iowa he was from. As it turned out, he lived not more than 30 minutes from where I grew up.

Early in the conversation he made it known that his daughter had died. He and his wife subsequently moved to their present home to be near her grave. I later learned that this all happened over five years earlier. As I listened, he unfolded his pain. A week before his daughter's fatal car wreck she had been date-raped and the dad felt he could have done something to prevent it. It became obvious to me that his ongoing guilt had suspended his grieving process in time, keeping it very much alive. I encouraged him to find someone he could talk it through with. He assured me a local pastor was available to him. As we parted, I felt sad that his guilt (whether imagined or real) prevented his soul from healing.

A DIFFERENT LOSS

The loss of a child carries very different connotations from the loss of a parent, sibling, or friend. Parents may even tell you that they wish it could have been them instead of their child that died. This feeling can haunt them for years. The pain after the loss of a child differs from any other loss of a person you may know and love. Accept this and acknowledge it where needed. Be very careful not to try to compare your loss of a job, marriage or pet with it.

Also, telling a grieving parent that their child "is in a better place" may be more of an insult than a comfort. Showing concern for the parent's pain is more helpful. A simple, "I have no idea of how bad you hurt but I am here for you" is much more supportive. You may even be able to offer to help them do something physical such as house work or cleaning the garage during difficult days. Inviting them to talk about their current thoughts about their child can be of help no matter how long it has been since the child's death.

ANGER

Anger can often be a part of the grieving process. In many cases it is even directed towards the deceased for leaving. Judith told me she felt a bit of anger towards her first husband for leaving her in death.

With the death of a child, anger isn't usually directed towards the child, but can be pointed to a third party.

Joy Swift, who lost three children through murder, explained anger expression in an article entitled "How to Survive the Death of a Child:"

> You will probably experience strong feelings of
> anger, especially if your child's death is caused
> by a particular person. In that case, you have
> someone to lash out at, if only in your mind.

But when the death is caused by accident or disease, your anger may become confused. You may pour it out on someone who is completely undeserving of it — a doctor, a police officer, a rescue worker, a friend, or even your spouse. I expressed my anger quite freely, but George, a passive man, kept his inside and talked to very few people about how he really felt. (*Signs of the Times* – December 1987)

TIME

Realizing the core emotional needs of one who has lost a child can be helpful in your ability to help them and understand what they are working through. These complications can add time to the normal grieving process; many parents actually grieve the loss of a child for years instead of months. This does not necessarily mean they are in need of professional counsel. An understanding, empathetic ear goes a long way in knowing what to say.

In the English language there is no word for a parent who has lost a child. There's a word for someone who lost a spouse — widow. There is a word for someone who has lost their parents — orphan. This lack of definition seems to be a reflection of the ambiguity of how parents who lose a child feel. Try to understand that and be careful not to try to explain it away. It's doubtful you will ever totally understand their feelings, unless you have indeed lost a child the same way as the one you are helping.

Beware of the tendency to pull away from people who are hurting emotionally. Watching a friend or relative work through emotions such as anger can be hard. Your presence can give them permission to express their hurt and be freer. Be free to tastefully talk about the lost child with them and invite their response. Trite comments like, "Well, you could always have (adopt) another child," may only multiply their hurts. Listen to where they are today in their feelings instead of referring to some possible "fix" in the future.

ADOPTION

Adoption is usually viewed as a very positive event. Placing a child in the arms of willing, loving parents is a good thing. The loss of a child to the birth parent, in many cases, is overlooked. The mother who offered that child for adoption, if she is alive, can often experience the grieving process either immediately or over the course of her life.

Louise chose adoption for her baby:

> It wasn't fair. I had morning sickness just like the other ladies. I had a large pregnant belly just like the other ladies. I was uncomfortable at night getting kicked in the ribs just like the other ladies. I went through the same pain of labor as the other ladies did. But it wasn't fair that I left the hospital empty-handed.
>
> Then another lady, that had never felt the pain and joy of pregnancy, walks into the

hospital empty-handed and walks out with a little pink bundle of joy.

My grieving was a choice. I knew I had to make a choice on how this child was going to be raised. Was I really ready to be a single parent? Or do I give this baby to a couple who is ready and waiting to be parents?

I struggled with that choice for almost eight months. In my heart, I knew adoption was the best for the baby. So the grieving started. The life growing inside wasn't for me to raise. I chose not to give into [*sic*] imaginations of sleeping with a baby on my chest, or playdates, having a child take their first steps to me. I was fortunate enough to have been attending counseling sessions at a crisis pregnancy center. There I was able to talk with other moms who placed their baby for adoption. I knew the most painful days were still yet ahead of me.

The pain of loss was real. It hurt! I cried! I went through pregnancy but my arms were empty!

That was many years ago, and yet there is a lump in my throat as I write this now. The pain of loss will always be felt, but for me, it's different as the years go by.

Louise's support for her grieving process only began in the days and weeks following the adoption. Those were critical times, to be sure. Reassurance for her decision was vital. Acknowledgment of her deep pain had to happen. Comments like, "Well, at least you won't have to potty train the baby," would be detrimental rather than helpful.

She would find more comfort in companionship, words of understanding, and even thoughtful opportunities to begin diverting her thoughts to her own healing. Like many situations where a child is lost, her pain is not something she will "get over" in a few months. It literally becomes a part of her. In the months, and even years ahead, it can be helpful to still speak of the child and give reassurance that the child is doing great.

DIVORCE

The process of a divorce affects the whole family. Symptoms of grief are often not associated with the process, but they are usually there. One of those issues can be the loss of children. This can be either through the physical separation or even through losing a child custody case.

Years after his divorce, Michael's former wife filed for full custody of their two teenage sons. He lost. Michael described his loss:

> My God, I am losing both my kids at once. Gone … across the country. I will never be a part of their day to day lives again. Everything I had is gone. I am now the

relatives they visit for a vacation. Every part of their lives that I participated in has now been severed irrevocably. Each time I see them the loss is displayed before my eyes. Changes in growth, physically, mentally, differences in attitudes … each time I see them they are different people, with shades and shadows of the kids I knew before. The kids I knew, the kids I raised, my sons … are gone. God, why not take my arms and legs, my eyes … why my kids? Take it all. Take everything I have. Leave my kids. Every text, every e-mail, every phone call, every Skype session, makes my loss more real. Reopening the wound, salt, alcohol, peroxide … They move on with their lives. Activities, sports, girls, learning to drive, prom, school … the calls get less, Skype sessions cease, texts are rarely returned because they have moved on with their lives leaving me behind. Anger, resentment, bitterness, hatred towards the one who caused this to occur, the one who uprooted them, the one who took them from all they knew and loved and moved them to a place with no friends and family other than the one who took them except on rare occasions. Everything points to the holes in your life. I coached them and their team… That's gone. The games, the plays, taking

them to their friends, running your life
around your kid's activities, everything
severed, cut off, burned ... lost. Emptiness ...
pain ....

Supporting a grieving parent who has experienced the loss of a child will feel unending. Your understanding will mean a lot. Be prepared to care for them through many emotional ups and downs and even some false starts in the recovery process. A non-critical ear may be just the thing they need most to make it through a moment or day of grief. Heart comments will often be more helpful than logical statements.

"I've never been where you are so I don't know exactly how you feel, but I would like to hear about your process of loss," can be a great way to help a hurting parent move towards a place of freedom.

ABORTION

The number of abortions in our society has risen drastically over the last several decades. It's been documented that emotional stress can be experienced, hence the growing pool of potential hurting men and women. If you are or know someone who has had an abortion either recently, or in the distant past, the grieving process is still very real. Like many losses, grief from an abortion can be "stuffed" down, embraced or spread out over a lifetime. Being aware of these options can help you be of great healing assistance to one experiencing it.

"I don't know how anyone could ever kill their baby," can be very hurtful or condemning when said in the presence of one who has experienced an abortion. Long-term sensitivity to grieving parents is a must. Helping someone in the depths of grieving an abortion will need to include concepts of forgiveness. Forgiveness may be needed from friends and relatives, from the unborn child, and even themselves. Understanding God's grace and forgiveness may be a beginning. Your understanding ear can be an important part of their victory.

MISCARRIAGE

One loss of a child that is often played down too much is that of a miscarriage. Friends and relatives can be cold or even rude by either ignoring the pain process or demanding one short-change the grieving process. We need to view this as a full-blown loss.

The mother in miscarriage cases does not suffer alone. The father can experience a variety of hurts that need to be processed. In his article "A Father's Story: Mourning the Baby We Never Had," Ian Wallach explained some responses he heard about:

> A month after the loss, I remembered each hushed backstory or confession of every male I knew who had experienced something similar, and I called them. A colleague whose wife had delivered a stillborn child offered to hang out and have a drink. A friend admitted that he felt embarrassed telling a coworker that he didn't want to attend a baby shower. Another, who lost his son in the 35th week,

told me that they'd moved apartments to escape the baby's room they had created. He said he took no time off from work — not a single day — yet still didn't understand why he'd misplace things or get lost in midsentence. After a pause, he asked me to keep a secret and said they were pregnant again but too frightened to tell anyone.

Your help for parents who have experienced a miscarriage needs to be long term. Allowing time alone to grieve helps, but don't be afraid to talk about it with them in months and even years later. A good suggestion you can make would be for the grieving parents to have a funeral. It will help a bit to bring closure for them. I also suggest you include the lost baby when referring to the number of children they have.

CHILDLESS

Mother's Day can be a hard day for some. Older, single people who would like to be married and have children but don't can view Mother's Day and Father's Day as a reminder of their personal disappointment and feelings of failure in the family area. The day that celebrates their missing role can trigger grief that doesn't seem to go away.

Shawn and Jenn are long-time friends of my family. Their life has been very fulfilled since their marriage many years ago, including a strong relationship with each other and a very productive career together in a religious non-profit organization. One thing is missing for them. They have no children.

Jenn offered some candid comments regarding their journey of hope and disappointment towards having children in their personal blog:

> It's complicated. And there's no time frame. The broken heart can't always be defined, but it's there. And the smallest little thing can stir it all back up. There's the lie that nobody cares and that people are tired of hearing about it. There's the lie that we'll be old and lonely and still aching for those six babies we never got to hold, raise: the legacy that never was. It's hard and it hurts. It's grief, loss, doubt, and sometimes guilt, smashed in some weird, oddly shaped box. A big part of the grieving process after IVF [in vitro fertilization] (x3) is knowing that you've done ALL you can using the most advanced medical treatments and procedures and surgeries. It's taking two steps towards closure, accepting that you will be 'the couple without kids,' and then falling backwards at the thought of Christmas mornings with just the two of us – forever.

MURDER AND SUICIDE

Violent deaths are always traumatic. In the event of a child's violent death, whether their life was taken by themselves or others, breadth is added to the sorrow. Horror and deep regret multiply the pain. The scope of this grief swells up as often unexplainable by many parents.

In an interview by Timothy C. Morgan on March 28, 2014, Kay Warren attempts to put her loss into words. She and her husband, Pastor Rick Warren, had lost a son to suicide one year earlier:

> Because of our love, we conceived a child together. I birthed him from my body. He was a part of me. A part of me is no longer here. How can I be the same? For us as a couple, as a family, there were five of us; now there are four. Our child murdered himself in the most raw way I can tell you. Suicide is self-murder. Our son, the murderer, was himself. The trauma of knowing what he did to himself, how he destroyed the body of this child that we loved. He did it to end the pain. How could we ever be the same? Trauma changes you. I can't ever go back to who I was. (*Christianity Today*)

As you come alongside parents in this form of grief, you will need to accept the fact that their hurt will be long term. In fact, you would be better prepared to help them if you expected their grief to increase for a time instead of subsiding. Beware of verbiage that pushes them to "get over it." The goal for a bereaved parent is getting through the process, not getting over it. Consolation of having other children, if this is true, is no comfort for the one lost.

Often simple statements of your continued friendship and support will do more good than attempts to make their hurt go away. Keep contact with them through social media and texting if impromptu visits seem out of place. Showing them your support will be more meaningful than saying it.

◈

« Point to Ponder »

Words of comfort need to revolve around the feelings of the bereaved, not the discomfort of the supporter.

WHAT TO SAY

WHAT NOT TO SAY

- ✓ **Tell me about your child/loved one. What was he/she like?**

    - ✗ *Your child is in a better place. God needed another angel.*

- ✓ **I miss him/her too.**

    - ✗ *You should be happy for the time you had with him/her.*

- ✓ **You did all you could do at the time.**

    - ✗ *How are you ever going to forgive yourself?*

- ✓ **I am praying for you and your family.**

    - ✗ *Well, at least you won't have to potty train that child.*

- ✓ **I have no idea of the depth of your pain but I am here for you.**

    - ✗ *You can always have/adopt other children.*

    - ✗ *You are lucky to at least have other children.*

Chapter 6

—

WHEN DEATH ROBS A FRIEND OR RELATIVE

*Helping those who have lost
someone close through death*

"I didn't want Grandpa to die," my cousin expressed through his tears. We were sitting in the back of the funeral home in rural Iowa. At seven years of age, I barely had an idea of what had happened. My grandpa was only 62 and his stroke was sudden. Since I did not feel close to him, I didn't experience the emotional loss. But the pain of those around me was evident, even to me.

TRAITS OF MOURNERS

Obviously, many factors affect the mourning process, such as age, definition of relationship, personality, type of loss and method of loss. In cases where loss is due to death (i.e., not relocation due to divorce, war or imprisonment) the grieving process can vary by whether the death was sudden, like my grandfather's, or over a protracted period of time such as in a terminal illness. The late Dr. Elisabeth Kubler-Ross observed that response to a terminal illness can include denial, bargaining, anger, acceptance and depression. In such cases, these "traits" may not show up in the griever's experience following the death of the loved one because they have been worked through before the death occurred. However, when death is sudden (as in my grandfather's case), those stages may be a part of the mourner's process.

Many hold firmly that everyone who experiences loss of any kind "must" go through stages or traits of the mourner as Dr. Kubler-Ross promoted. However, not everyone agrees. Dr. James E. Means in his book, *A Tearful Celebration*, expresses his disagreement:

> It doesn't do any good to analyze grief intellectually as the scholars do. An objective, cool discussion of the meaning or stages of the grief experience is worthless, and possibly even harmful to the grief-stricken. Nothing has been quite so objectionable or distasteful to me in recent months as the feeling that I am being scrutinized by those trying to determine what

"stage" of grief is current or what progress I have made toward 'wholeness.' The feeble, and sometimes ridiculous, attempts to compartmentalize grief and dissect it academically are offensive to me as I live daily with the personal odyssey of pain. (pg. 52)

NEED TO GRIEVE

It is very important to realize the need for grief at some level regardless of the definition of your relationship with the relative lost. Some try to minimize this with the logic that they weren't married to that person or "he was just an uncle and not my dad." The freedom to grieve is needed nonetheless. Many times, the best thing to do is to give the person permission to mourn. Zig Ziglar has been quoted as saying; "If there were no love, there'd be no grief." Help them realize that grief is not a sign of weakness, but simply the recognition that they have lost someone they love.

"I don't know what's going on inside me, though" she finally admitted. "It's like I am painfully remembering Judith along with my mother."

"Oh, I see what is going on now," I responded. "I noticed that when you visited Judith before she died that you 'kept a stiff upper lip' and no tears. Now that this other emotionally-charged event has happened, it is bringing up that unresolved grief to be processed. That is good."

"That explains it perfectly. Now I know I am not crazy," came her relieved comment.

The individual I spoke with was a very close friend to my wife. Now, a year later, she had experienced a very emotional event in her marriage (that turned out positively). The reason she called me was that she did not see how the emotion of the present situation was connected to the feelings of loss she still had for Judith and also her mother.

Her story is a great example of undealt-with grief that was "stuffed" down and not released will resurface later. It does not go away. The next time a deeply emotional event happens in one's life, it can come back for processing. It is very important that we all be alert to our own personal grief and process it fully.

A NEW PART

The pain of grieving a loss never really goes away. It simply becomes a part of you.

I experienced this truth at the memorial service of a friend who died in his 30s. Of course, I was saddened for the families' loss at the outset of the service, but wasn't totally prepared for how the events of that time would affect me. Twice during that celebration my tears flowed freely. The first time was when Luke, his 10-11-year-old son, cried openly. As I watched and heard him miss his dad, I felt his pain from deep inside.

I reflected as to why this response came from me. Two possibilities came to mind. First, one of my sons was 10-11 years old when I told him his mom had died and held him on my lap for a time of sobbing. However, my second option is what really took place. I was that 10-11- year-old boy 53 years ago! My dad had died suddenly in his 30s and it was ME that truly had experienced the emotions Luke displayed. Watching him brought back that part of me that had hurt similarly so long ago. It was a part of me...down deep. And it was okay.

As I've stated many times, it behooves us to realize the reality of grief, deal with it properly and help those we know to do the same.

GUILT

Steph began having bad neck and headaches months after her mother-in-law died. She went to several doctors to no avail. Sleep became an elusive thing. At the same time she found herself rehearsing the events surrounding her mother-in-law's death. Steph reviewed her actions in response to the news of her terminal illness. "Had I done enough? Did I believe Mom would be healed strongly enough? Was my lack, in any way, responsible for her death?" These questions, and others, came back to mind from time to time, causing deep guilt.

Eighteen months after her loss, Steph was in a church service praying, all the while feeling the heavy weight of guilt. A person new to the church standing next to her leaned over and said, "God wants you to know that your conscience is free before Him." She asked him to repeat his comment. As the full depth of this profound statement descended, her headache pain vanished permanently. No more guilt.

The closeness of the relative who has died will affect the level of loss felt. The loss of a parent can leave a person feeling abandoned, even orphaned, whereas the loss of a distant relative may cause one's grief to be marginalized instead of fully realized. In any case, talking through one's feelings with a person who is not trying to "fix" them can be of great help.

THINGS TO DO

In the event that one's relationship has not been close, often deep feelings don't dominate the griever's experience. Their loss, however, should not be minimized. A friend of mine lost a cousin a couple of years ago. She felt the loss of her cousin's friendship and love but did not experience "deep" mourning like others. She did come up with an idea that gave her comfort. She bought a couple rose bushes and asked that they be planted in her cousin's honor. I know of another man who found it hard to show his feelings when his mother died so, to express his loss, he put up a memorial arrangement in her honor for the public to see.

Thoughtful offers that can help a person express their feelings may include the following: "Can I help you do something in memory of your loved one?" or "Have you considered writing your loved one a symbolic letter to tell them how much you miss them?"

Understanding the depth of the relationship between the griever and the one they lost will give you a better idea of what to say. Thoughtful comments similar to the following can be very beneficial to the griever: "Is there something I can help you do in memory of your loved one?" or "May I go with you to a grief recovery meeting sometime?"

FREEDOM TO EXPRESS

About 18 months after my wife, Ruth, died, my mother died. Then about 18 months after Mom's death, my grandmother (her mother) died. I noticed that one of my brothers did not express his grief much at our mother's funeral. Then, just before our grandmother's funeral he suddenly broke down emotionally and sobbed for the longest time. I went to him with a big hug. Upon regaining composure he wisely said, "Well, I guess I really needed to get that out." I concurred. The Scots have a saying that "some things are better felt than tell't." Grief can be like that at times. We can aid mourners by helping them allow for that expression of pain in whatever way fits their situation.

Meaningful conversation about the person lost can be very helpful. Beware of faulty thinking that saying the name of the deceased will add to their pain, because in reality it helps relieve it. Using the loved one's name in conversation with a griever often opens the door to expressing their emotion and pain, which can encourage the slow healing process required in mourning. They are probably thinking about them anyway. By you mentioning their name, it gives them permission to express it.

NO TIME FRAME

One of the things I have observed about grieving the loss of a relative when it is not a spouse or child revolves around the tendency to spread the grieving process out over a longer period of time.

The months following Judith's death were filled with my experiences of going through the grieving process completely. Since my life was so changed on a daily basis with her gone I "leaned into" the process, fully engulfed in dealing with working through my pain and redefining my life every day. My eight children, however, returned to their daily life routines with all the schedules and responsibilities that go with young families. By sheer logistics they had to focus more on doing life and, in many ways, set aside the loss of their mother for much of their day. That does not mean they didn't mourn. They all did that well. It simply implies that they had to deal with their grief in shorter spurts of remembering their mom. This 'spreading it out' process translated into grieving over a longer period of time. Time for the grieving process can thus be longer when a relative is lost and we should exercise understanding towards them.

My experience of concentrating on my grief was similar after Ruth died. I intentionally experienced my mourning and even sought out counselors who had "been there, done that." Ruth's close friend from nursing school did not have that opportunity. Following Ruth's death she had to daily get her kids off to school and go back to work at the hospital. I spoke with her over a year later. In that conversation I realized her sense of loss for Ruth was still very, very fresh. The next year I visited her and her husband. At that time, again, I realized she was still missing Ruth as if she had died the month before. A busy life had forced her to put her grieving "on hold" much of the time. This did not diminish the fact that she needed to process her grief. It just determined how long it took to do it.

THE FIRSTS

In most grieving experiences the "firsts" are significant. The first holiday, the first birthday, or even the first visit with common friends and family after a loss can be hard and/or healing. One great way to help mourners you know could be to remember these times with them. Often a call, card or visit in memory of their lost loved one can go a long way in helping them heal. Don't wait or even expect them to ask for this. They may not even realize how these times can blindside one emotionally after a loss.

YOUR RELATIONSHIP

If you are on the list of common friends or relatives of one who has lost a close relative, you might consider reassuring the griever that your relationship with them remains stable. Following Ruth's death, one of her best friends was in our Sunday school class. At the funeral they made it clear that "if I ever needed anything" they would be there. However, I noticed that they slowly pulled away from me. A couple of years later I even called to arrange to visit them and they turned me down. Often losing a relative can cause uncertainties in other relationships. You can help by being very proactive in reassuring them that your relationship with them continues secure.

HONESTY

Honesty is the best policy. If you have not experienced the same loss as the person you are seeking to help, don't say you understand. It would be better to simply ask them what it is like. Leading questions also help true expression to come. Pretending to sympathize doesn't help anyone. Empathy goes farther. Statements like, "It must be hard to lose your mom," are received easier than fake sympathy or saying things that don't come from real experience. Feeble attempts to relate such as, "I know how you feel. I lost a kitten once," will not be of much help.

Demanding a grieving friend or relative stop or "get over" their grief seldom works. To begin with, it is important to keep in mind that grieving evolves as a variable process and not an event. A much better response to a mourner's needs would be, "How can I help you move past your present pain?" Sometimes this will require you to get close to their lives in order to discern small ways you can help them.

Aiding someone who has experienced a loss may require a little extra effort. You may even need to work through your own fear of pain to come alongside the griever who needs to press on to a winning position.

HOW TO HELP

Friends who began to show concern for MY pain helped me the most as time passed. Comments like, "You must hurt deeply," were better than comments that tried to diminish my pain. Those who wish to help the mourner need to realize that time and conversation do more to healing than a lecture. Anne Cetas is quoted as saying, "When someone's grieving — listen, don't lecture."

Gaining a better understanding of the process of the

grievers in your life will be of great benefit to their healing. Coming through the grieving period as a winner can be even more definite when one has helpful friends and counselors to aid them instead of pulling away too soon.

Months after my wife, Judith, died, I received many requests to share things I had learned in my grieving process to that point in my life. These experiences were helpful for me and, I found, very helpful to others as well. It hit me one day after a couple of these events that I should not "hoard my lessons." It was that thought that prompted me towards writing this book to help others. Dag Hammarskjöld has been quoted as saying, "We cannot afford to forget any experience, even the most painful."

Many well-meaning friends tried to say things to me that would push my grief pain away too soon. Granted, moving past the pain of loss becomes what the process is all about. The problem comes in trying to stuff it or "forget" it and lose the lessons. These lessons can be of great benefit to you, as well as to others. The loss and the grieving process become a part of the bereaved person's life — not an experience to be forgotten. Helping them digest their experiences and feelings is much healthier than trying to help them forget.

You could help the one you are escorting through their loss by encouraging them to write down their experiences and feelings today so they can remember and use them later. Offering to help develop a scrapbook, photo album, or slide show of the loved one as a memorial can also be helpful. It can be comforting to feel like there are ways to help people to not forget their loved one.

Writing a "grief letter" of any kind helps some find closure for their pain. I found an example of the "grief letter" recently while sorting through my files. I came across a letter written by one of my daughters to her mother months after she had died. In it my daughter simply described the events and process of her pain after her mom died. Of course, this letter was never sent. It couldn't be. However, the simple expression gave release.

At some point, to bring closure to their pain, you might suggest this idea to the person for whom you are caring.

GET INVOLVED

Helping someone who has experienced the loss of a spouse may take commitment that goes beyond a "word" or single act.

Following the loss of her first husband, Judith struggled with keeping life's decisions on course. She not only lost her husband, but she also had the duties of the home and the care of four young boys. Three couples in her circle of friends responded by forming a committee to help her with life decisions relating to her family and finances. This practical help became the stabilizer she needed most at that stage in her life. She received help from her advisory council for several years.

Not all aids for the bereaved need to be continued for years. However, we do need to think beyond just offering one-time helps. Again, relief for grief is not a quick fix, but rather it is an acknowledgement of the pain and support for the process, whether emotional or physical in nature.

◈

« Point to Ponder »

The grieving are not looking for logic
statements of being told what to do.
What they need is a listening ear.

WHAT TO SAY

WHAT NOT TO SAY

✓ **His/her memory will live on in my heart.**

    ✗ *His/her time was up. His/her death was meant to be.*

✓ **Can I take the kids to the zoo on Saturday?**

    ✗ *(say nothing and avoid all contact)*

✓ **I have been remembering you a lot lately and I love you.**

    ✗ *You are lucky to have had them in your life for as long as you did.*

✓ **I know he/she loved/relied on you a lot.**

    ✗ *At least they had a good life.*

✓ **He/she knew how much you loved him/her.**

    ✗ *I understand your pain. I lost someone once.*

    ✗ *You need to only remember the good and forget all the bad.*

Chapter 7

—

WHEN KIDS GRIEVE

*Insight and help for aiding
the immature who need to mourn*

Sugar Bear, a medium-sized house dog, joined our family when my kids were small. One day a negative thing happened between Sugar Bear and an already troublesome neighbor. I knew we could no long keep Sugar Bear as our pet. So, I proceeded to tell my kids that Sugar Bear would have to go live with someone else. My older daughter began to cry. I went with my first instinct. I commanded her to hush and stop crying immediately. WRONG! It wasn't till much later in life I realized that I was not teaching her a healthy way of dealing with her loss. Instead, it would have been better had I held her through her tears and said, "It's okay to cry."

Eleven years after that event I was faced with the horrid

task of telling my children that their mommy had died that morning.

Ruth died early in the morning while the kids were still asleep. Two nurses, both friends from church, were helping with Ruth's care that morning. I watched Ruth take her last breath, said good-bye and sobbed uncontrollably. My next attention had to be regarding the children. I decided to not tell the kids yet. I wanted to spare them the terror of watching their mother's lifeless body being carried from the house. So, I closed the bedroom door and proceeded with the morning's normal routine.

YOUR MOMMY DIED

I got the kids off to school and then made the necessary calls to the doctor and then the funeral home. Finally, with the bedroom empty, I called the school to arrange to come get my four children. We rode home in silence. Upon arriving in our driveway, I turned to my somber kids and began. "You know that Mom has been very sick for a long time. Well, this morning she died and went to heaven. We now have to go on without her." As my kids began to weep, silently at first, I reached for my 11-year-old and pulled him into my lap for a sobbing session.

We continued to sit quietly for what seemed like hours. Finally, I suggested we go in the house. Each child went to their own room. Understanding the importance of openly expressing and dealing with loss, I was not satisfied with the silent sobbing session we had had in the van. Methodically, I went to each child's room and talked to them about the meaning and implications of their mother's death. I wanted them each to have the private freedom to cry and to see me cry in front of them. And I did. Of course, the way I talked to each was age specific, but effective. I began, as best I could, to monitor each child's mourning process.

I was blunt about the obvious, pointing out that she was gone and that we would have to go on in life without her. It would be difficult to live without her and it really hurt.

I did not shield the kids from the closure process. They went with me to pick out a casket for their mom. They stood by me at the viewing to watch and receive comfort from friends. They walked with me down the aisle of the church in front of the casket at her funeral. I watched as friends and relatives gave attention to them and not just me during comforting visits. We talked about her around the table for months. Our family photo albums became much more valuable.

AGE SPECIFIC

It can be a mistake to assume a small child has no idea about death. They hear it referred to in conversation, movies and from friends. Children learn how to respond to life's events by watching the adults around them. However, how one talks to a pre-teen is different than a 5-year-old. The Hungarian psychologist, Maria Nagy, has explored the meaning of death for children of different ages. At ages three to five, they deny that death is final; it is like sleep, or like a parent going to work or on a brief vacation. Between five and nine, children accept the idea that someone has died, but not until age of ten do they understand that they themselves must die. (*The Harvard Medical School Journal*)

My youngest was eleven when his mom died. I believe he mourned as best as he could at his age. About ten years later something happened that took us both by a bit of surprise. By this time he was married.

We all had moved from the state where Ruth's grave is located. Life had moved on. Aaron had lived through the loss, the blending of two families, completion of schooling and marriage. He and his wife had even worked for a funeral home company. They traveled through Michigan and decided to stop to visit Ruth's grave. As Aaron stared at his mom's marker he suddenly burst into sobs. He had mourned her death as a child. Now he mourned his loss as an adult.

THINGS THAT HELP

Helping a child cope with a loss due to death can be fundamental in helping them deal with loss of any kind the rest of their life.

Sandra Aldrich lost her husband when her two children were small. She recorded her observations and experiences in her book *Living Through the Loss of Someone You Love*. "The most important thing we can do for a grieving child is to talk to him—and listen to his observations. Children have many questions they often can't articulate. But a concerned adult can help them sort through conflicting emotions." (pg. 195)

Sandra goes on in chapter six of her book to provide helpful bullet points in dealing with children and loss:

- Tell the child right away
- Be truthful
- Tell only what the child can handle
- Encourage children to express feelings
- Allow children to attend the funeral
- Take the child to the cemetery
- Let the child talk
- Encourage communication
- Be there for them
- Affirm the child's feelings

ADULTS ARE KEY

Helping a child mourn can be an uncertain thing to do. Variables include the age of the child, the relationship they had with their loss, and how that child sees the adults in their life deal with loss. One big mistake would be to avoid the subject of their loss with some idea that silence brings healing. It does not. Kids don't always know how to think about hard things or how to respond. Adults play a key part of helping them mourn well. One cannot wait for the child to open up and talk about it. Often, a caring prompt to talk by a trusted adult breaks the silent barrier between hurt and healing.

Honesty about death is a must. Comments like, "Grandpa is asleep," can only increase a child's uncertainties. Openly expressing your own feelings in forms resembling, "I am going to really miss Grandpa a lot," and "I cry when I think of Grandpa," can be helpful in showing the child how to mourn.

Your concern for a grieving child can be converted to help with loving encounters where the child is free to respond to their loss. Often, someone not so close to the situation is more successful helping a child than loved ones. My oldest son was finishing high school when his mom died. His friend's parents were great helpers to him during the first year after Ruth died. They would hug him and say things like, "Your mom would be proud of you." Or, "It must be hard missing your mom."

Beware about adding embarrassment to the child's grief by somehow forcing them to grieve in front of people they don't feel comfortable around. Unlike my action concerning Sugar Bear, don't require the child to stifle her sorrow. Like adults, creating a "memorial" for the lost loved one such as drawing a picture, writing a letter or even putting together their own photo album can be beneficial to a child. Remember the child's age when discussing grieving. Adults should not confide in a child too deeply concerning their own grieving process.

The day Judith died we had 24 grandchildren. Each one was given opportunity to physically come to our house, say goodbye to her, and mourn her leaving with their parents. In addition to that, I asked one of my daughters to put together and print a photo book that included a page dedicated to pictures of Judith with each of the grandkids, one page per grandkid. These were given to each grandchild at Christmas (3 months later). Many of the grandchildren would look at that book nightly for months afterwards. It was more than a memorial, it was a grieving aid.

◈

« Point to Ponder »

Comfort for the grieving needs to be
more directed to their pain than the
one they have lost.

WHAT TO SAY

WHAT NOT TO SAY

✓ **Your hurt must be big right now.**

    ✗ *Grandpa is sleeping.*

✓ **(say nothing but give a hug)**

    ✗ *Keep your happy face on.*

✓ **What was it like when...?**

    ✗ *Life must go on.*

✓ **I love you and am proud of you.**

    ✗ *Now you are the head/leader of your house.*

✓ **I loved him/her too and will miss him/her.**

    ✗ *God needed him/her in heaven.*

✓ **Can I help you write a letter about your loss/grief?**

    ✗ *You must not speak ill of the dead.*

    ✗ *You are the man (woman) of the house now...buck up.*

"Like one who takes away a garment on a cold day,
or like vinegar poured on soda,
is one who sings songs to a heavy heart."
PROVERBS 25:20

Chapter 8

—

WHEN BARRIERS AFFECT MOURNING

Gender difference
tips for helpers

Men tend to replace while women process. There may be some truth to that statement but hopefully it is not always the case. Men need to process their grief as well. Then there is the time factor to consider. Generally, men can take from 6 to 18 months to process their grief, whereas women tend to take one to two years to gain relief. No set time requirement exists. Each person grieves differently.

I received an email from a friend who lost his wife suddenly about five months earlier, asking me about how I found a new life's partner following my wife's death. What do

I say? Do I encourage him to press on in looking for a replacement or do I recommend he wait longer?

My comments to my friend included an honest reply with my evaluation of my own grieving process which required nine months before I felt like I could be able to love again romantically.

An audience I spoke to the year after Judith's death numbered over one thousand. "What have you learned through your mourning process?" was the topic requested. Following the closing remarks a long line formed to chat with me. I observed a very notable difference with this lineup — the large number of men in line. In previous years I noticed a common trend for ladies, dominantly, to chat with me when the topic had an emotional expression. This time nearly half of those in line were men who had lost a spouse. From many of the men, one of the comments I repeatedly heard included, "It was refreshing to hear someone express what I have been going through." I also realized the conversations with the men were different in nature than those with the widowed ladies in line.

One of the ladies from the audience approached me with a smile through her tears. She immediately began by telling me her story. She told a couple of examples that depicted her journey since her husband died. It was obvious there was a sense of connection between what I had shared and her experiences.

MEN HEAR MEN

Behind her was a square jawed gentleman with a military haircut. A tear glistened in his eye. When our hands touched he simply said, "I almost didn't come this morning. I'm glad I did. You ministered to me." I replied briefly. His lip began to quiver and he turned to walk away. I later learned that there were over six men in that audience who had lost their wives in the previous year. He was one of them.

That experience accentuated a casual observation I made years before. Men and women tend to process grief differently. After Ruth's death I sought out other men who had lost their wives to talk to about my journey. I actually tried to be careful about talking to widows because of the possibility of the meeting being viewed as inappropriate. One of my observations included that women often invited conversations about their grief where men simply acknowledged it when asked.

THE CHEMISTRY

Besides normal observation, an article in the *Journal of Psychosomatic Research* (1987;31[3]:375-83) entitled, "Sex Differences in Prolactin Change During Mourning" recounted a study on why there seems to be such a difference between men and women and their grieving. A team of scientists reported the following results giving credence to chemical differences between the sexes:

> Fourteen men and 12 women were interviewed eight weeks after conjugal bereavement to discuss the events prior to the spouse's death and the subsequent bereavement period. Prolactin (PRL) was

measured at the beginning and end of the interview. Descriptions of the deceased spouse were obtained during the interview and rated for Developmental Level of Object Representation (DLOR), a measure of the cognitive complexity of the description. There were significant correlations between DLOR and PRL change for both men and women but the correlation for women was positive and the correlation for men was negative. These findings extend the literature on the psychological correlates of PRL change and suggest that the physiological changes associated with mourning are different for men and women.

JUST THE FACTS

Many times men will simply rehearse the facts as a form of processing their feelings.

My phone rang exposing an out-of-state area code I was not familiar with. "Is this Dave Knapp?" was the reply to my "hello." "This is Bob," came his response to my affirmative reply. I instantly knew who it was. A mutual friend had informed me that Bob's second wife had died a couple of weeks earlier. Bob was responding to my email requesting a time to talk.

Our one-hour talk (I should say listen, on my part) reviewed the entire set of circumstances to his wife's passing.

He reviewed her medical history leading up to her death as well as the details of the day she died. I listened.

DON'T ASSUME

The conversation extended to the days and weeks since her memorial service. One familiar issue Bob referred to and expounded upon was how so many people told him about their perception of his mourning experience without really talking to him enough to know where he was in the process. One commenter expressed, "Your anger is normal." He pointed out to me that he had not experienced anger to date and their comment came across to him as demeaning.

I found similar comments by well-meaning friends during my losses to be accusative when an informative approach would have been better. Instead of assuming Bob's experience of anger at that stage of his grieving, it would have been easier to deal with had they taken the time to listen to him and find out what aspect of mourning he was experiencing at the time.

MORE MEN

In the last decade the number of single men over the age of 65 has increased by 21%, due in part to the closing gap in the life expectancy of men and women. (Perry Garfinkl, *New York Times*) With this increase of men who have experienced loss returning to singleness, what do we say to them?

Many of the books on the grieving process relate to the experiences of mostly women in their mourning journey. Recommendations such as "Tell me how you are feeling this week," may be responded to with a lengthy, tearful explanation from a lady. The response you get from a man may be more to the point. He may answer with one or two sentences and change the subject. To a man you may be more helpful by asking him what things he has done that week to remember or commemorate his loved one. He may find more healing by simply rehearsing the facts involved either before or after his loss.

In the months following Ruth's death, I recall vividly wishing that someone would ask me, "Could you tell me how your wife died? What was it like that day?" I sensed I would have found great relief rehearsing the events of that fateful day. No one did.

Ruth Davis Konigsberg wrote an article entitled, "5 Surprising truths about Grief" for AARP (March 14, 2011). In it, she pointed out some contrasts between men and women in grieving the loss of a spouse:

> **Loss is harder for men.** For years, clinicians have been operating under the assumption that women grieve harder and longer than men. In 2001, psychologists Wolfgang and Margaret Stroebe (a husband-and-wife team) decided to examine all the existing research and came to the surprising conclusion that, after taking into account the higher rate of depression in the overall female population, men actually suffer more from being bereaved. We might be under the impression

that widows despair more, but that's because there are many more widows to observe.

WOMEN EXPRESS FEELINGS

While women who lose their husbands often speak of feeling abandoned or deserted, widowers tend to experience the loss "as one of dismemberment, as if they had lost something that kept them organized and whole," Michael Caserta, chairman of the Center for Healthy Aging at the University of Utah, said by e-mail.

Men often struggle in sharing their deep feelings, especially negative ones. So, while it is effective to ask a lady how she is feeling after the death of someone close, it would be more productive to ask a man, "How has your daily routine changed?" Then if they don't have any ideas, you could suggest some things for them to do in working through their grief.

HELPING BOTH

Any loss due to death is a difficult experience. Often, one good way to help people process their grief is to assist them in validating the life of the one gone.

I saw a great example of this being put into practice at a memorial service I attended. A half sheet of paper was provided as an insert in the memorial service bulletin. It was blank except for the title, *"The Gift of Memories."* During the service, an announcement was given and a few minutes of silence provided for attenders to write something about the deceased for the family to have and read later. I observed many people filling it out.

Another very helpful suggestion would be to offer to help the bereaved in putting together a photo slide show, photo album or scrapbook about the one they have lost. This can be helpful to the "immediate" relatives, such as the spouse and children, but also to others who loved them. Some have even planted a tree or rose garden in memory of their lost friend or relative.

LONELINESS

One of the ground-leveling traits in grief for both men and women is dealing with suffocating loneliness. Both struggle with this one.

The year our youngest son, Aaron, entered kindergarten, my wife and I made efforts to prepare him for the traumatic event of being away from Mom for the whole day. On one occasion, Ruth was walking hand-in-hand with him near our house. She reviewed the fun Aaron would have the next week at school all day. Suddenly, Aaron stopped and burst into tears. Ruth inquired about his crying. Through his wrinkled face he blurted, "Mom, then YOU will be home all ALONE?"

Loneliness can be devastating. Often, a person who is grieving struggles with that as much or more than dealing with the actual loss. It will help you relate with your grieving friends and relatives if you can keep that aspect of grieving in mind, especially when their grieving results from a loss due to death. An honest question of, "How are you coping with your loneliness?" can go a long way in showing empathy.

BE SPECIFIC

I mentioned earlier that I had several well-meaning friends offer, "Dave, any time you want to talk just call me. I mean it, anytime." In all honesty, it was a great help when a friend called and said, "Dave, do you want to go for a walk at the reservoir at 8 tomorrow morning, or Friday at 7 AM?" My experience concluded that generalities seldom happen but specifics do. You may not be able to relate with much of the grieving process, but if you break it down a bit, you can probably relate some to loneliness. Saying something specific about helping them deal with their loneliness, even for one day, will go much further than soothing your conscience with a generality that probably won't materialize.

INSTRUMENTAL MOURNERS

Men tend to be more *instrumental mourners* who experience and speak of their grief intellectually and physically. They are most comfortable with seeking accurate information, analyzing facts, making informed decisions and taking action to solve problems. Remaining strong, dispassionate and detached in the face of powerful emotions, they may speak of their grief in an intellectual way, thus appearing to others as cold, uncaring and without feeling.

Asking men, "What have you done to memorialize (remember) your wife?" or "Can I help you do something to memorialize your wife's life?" can be of benefit to them.

INTUITIVE MOURNERS

Women, on the other hand, may tend towards being *intuitive mourners* who experience a full, rich range of emotions in response to grief. Comfortable with strong emotions and tears, they are sensitive to their own feelings and to the feelings of others as well. Since they feel strong emotions so deeply, they're less able to rationalize and intellectualize the pain of grief, and more likely to appear overwhelmed and devastated by it.

Being sensitive with questions like, "How have your feelings of loss been evident this week?" or "Where are you in your pain level today?" can show concern for how she is doing.

MOURNING IS LEARNED

More and more research has emerged to help us know how to help both men and women in the grieving process. The *Mourning Matters Ministry* gives helpful insight in their Spring 2013 quarterly newsletter:

> Though we are hard-wired to grieve, how we mourn is a learned response. Mourning is the outward expression of internal grief. It is how we choose to adapt and cope, or in some cases not adapt or cope. There are many ways someone can mourn the death of a loved one. Men and women tend to mourn in different ways. Women tend to like to talk, to cry, to express themselves emotionally and to have someone validate what they are going through.

Men on the other hand tend to be more cognitive. They may like to be involved in activities that honor their loved one. New research now suggests that laughter is as much a part of the mourning process as crying is, for in laughter we give ourselves small moments of rest.

After Louise surrendered her baby to adoptive parents (see chapter 5), her counselor wisely suggested that she rent some comedy movies in the following weeks to give her emotions a bit of a break in the mourning process over the loss of the baby. She did, and it worked.

GRIEVING IS DIFFERENT

"Because grieving is so individual," explains Elizabeth W.D. Groves in her booklet *"Becoming A Widow"* (New Growth Press, 2012), "it is hard for others to know what is most helpful for them to do or say…. For example, some widows find that seeing their husband's clothes in the closet is very painful, so it feels good to clear out those clothes as soon as possible. Other widows find it comforting to have their husband's clothes still there, so they want to keep some of them around for a time." (pgs. 12, 13)

In addition to increasing your awareness of the general characteristics of the mourning process, you can also be a better friend to the griever by understanding some gender distinctives in the mourning process. The effectiveness of your assistance can increase in pointing your friend towards a road to victory over the pain of their grief.

« Point to Ponder »

Theological lectures are seldom of much relief for the pain of new grief.

WHAT TO SAY

WHAT NOT TO SAY

✓ **I wish I had the right words. I just want you to know I care.**

> ✗ *I don't want to hear details. I just want you better.*

✓ **Can I come by Wednesday evening to visit?**

> ✗ *Wow. You look sad/awful.*

✓ **I can't take away your pain but I can be a friend.**

> ✗ *You need to keep a stiff upper lip.*

✓ **Have things happened to ease your pain?**

> ✗ *I could NEVER go through what you are right now.*

✓ **What have you done to deal with your grief/loss?**

> ✗ *Now that she/he is dead, you should get a pet.*

"One often calms one's grief by recounting it."

PIERRE CORNEILLE

Chapter 9

—

WHEN CULTURE SHADES GRIEVING

Cross-culture difference
tips for helpers

In today's world many of us are multi-cultural in a number of ways. You may find yourself interacting with people from different cultural backgrounds through work, church, clubs, your kids' schools or even where you live. It would be presumptuous to conclude that all people grieve the same. All humans grieve, but how they do it can be based on teaching, religion, worldview or their own observations. Even if you disagree with their methods of grieving, the early mourning process is not the time to criticize them or to educate them to what you consider a better way. Your best plan would be to simply help them grieve well and then be open to help them if they have questions about their own perspective versus yours at a later, less emotional time.

KARAJA TRIBESMEN

I traveled to a very remote part of central Brazil visiting missionary outposts. While there, I witnessed two different approaches to grieving. The first one happened in the semi-civilized tribal village of the Karaja. One of the tribal elders had crossed the river in his six-foot, standup canoe to drink beer in the town bar. Late at night, on his return attempt to home, he fell in the river and drowned. I arrived on the village side of the river shortly after they pulled his body from the muddy water. I observed that no one was weeping. Many were whispering, but there was no deep emotional expression. They just did not do that there. The only emotion revealed seemed to be a worried look on the faces of a few women as they held a clinched fist to their mouths.

A few days later, back across the river in the small Brazilian town, I witnessed another death scene. There in the sun-drenched town a processional of kids dressed in white were accompanying a small coffin. I asked the missionaries to explain what I was seeing. They informed me that a child under the age of two had died and was being buried that day. No adults walked with the coffin. In fact, the child probably had no name. The town's people believed that a baby did not have a "soul" till about age two so the baby was not considered a real person until then, when it was given a name. Since, in their minds, this infant was not a real person, no adults bothered to mourn for its loss, not even the parents.

DIVERSITY

The concept of grieving a loss due to death often can be affected by the cultural perception about death itself. This varies from country to country as well as from sub-cultures within those countries. Finlo Rohrer published an article in the BBC News Magazine (2010) entitled, *"How Much Can You Mourn a Pet?"* In it, he admits, "The UK has what is seen by many non-Britons as a slightly repressed attitude towards death." Other European countries tend to have reputations for emphasizing death (i.e. the vampire stories).

THE GROUP EFFECT

Grief in a culture grows from a society and belief system that prizes and cultivates individual experience. Some languages have no equivalent to the term *grief*. In parts of Japan, the concept of emotions that are solely expressed on the part of an individual are not common. In those societies, individual identity is a function of social and communal harmony. A harmonized atmosphere as part of a family or community is sensed among the members. Personal grief is therefore more of a shared event.

In some traditional Chinese cultures, death presents the problem of pollution as understood in terms of their religious world view. One of the purposes of funeral rituals is to protect the men from that pollution, while on the other hand the women take the pollution on themselves. In turn, this practice results in purifying the deceased for the next life. Other than mourning, any other practices revolving around death would seem to be culture-specific. Death presents pollution or powerlessness in some cultural contexts as much as it presents separation, loss and sometimes trauma in the modern West.

THE INDIVIDUAL EFFECT

Western individuals, on the other hand, who successfully come to terms with a traumatic death, may change how they think about themselves, how they relate to others, and how they view life in general. As our world changes and becomes more of a worldwide community, so views on death evolve. Changes experienced by individuals in other cultures might be just as wide-ranging but cover spheres not experienced in the West.

When something important happens in individuals' lives, they do not just think about it; they talk about it with others. Grief and mourning do not just happen inside a person; they happen in the interactions between people. In most cultures throughout human history, myth and ritual provide the intersubjective space in which one can construct the meaning of the deceased's life, death and influence over the survivors' lives. Understanding these concepts can give direction in how to talk to the bereaved. Conversations about the definition of the relationship lost can validate the lost life and aid the mourner in processing their own pain of loss.

One cross-cultural project sought to compare the rules about the emotional expression of grief. Anthropologist Unni Wikan, for example, compared the rules in Egypt and Bali, both Islamic cultures. She found that in Bali, women were strongly discouraged from crying, while in Egypt women were considered abnormal if they did not incapacitate themselves in demonstrative weeping.

Asking a grieving friend from another culture what their traditional methods are can be one way to show concern and empathy. This gives you a chance to at least acknowledge their hurts whether they are the same as yours or not.

PRACTICES

The traditional Jewish culture found in the Old Testament of the Bible had many practices continued in many places today. Even though their existence revolved around their God, the expression of grief in the time of severe loss revealed their human experience. Weeping, a primary indication of grief, was referred to a great deal. Time (30-70 days) was set aside to mourn deeply. The physical appearance of the mourners was altered to indicate their condition. Ashes or outer garments often symbolized a grieving heart. The realization of the gift of the presence of friends and family regularly induced comfort. (The Holman Bible Dictionary, 1991)

Judaism today calls for a period of intense mourning known as shiva that lasts seven days after a loved one is buried. After shiva, most normal activities can be resumed, but it is the end of sheloshim that marks the completion of religious mourning for a spouse.

LIVING IN ANOTHER CULTURE

Cross-cultural effects on how one mourns also come in other packages besides historical traditions. Families living abroad, outside of their home country and culture can be very confused about the mourning process. Jonathan Trotter addresses this confusion in his article *"Outlawed Grief, a Curse Disguised"* (December 22, 2013):

> Living abroad is an amazing adventure, but it comes with some baggage. And sometimes, the baggage fees are hidden, catching you by surprise, costing more than you planned. You thought you had it all weighed out, you could handle this, squeeze right under the limit.
>
> But then it got heavy. Your new friends moved away, or your child's new friend moved away. Far away. Like other continents away. And your kid's broken heart breaks yours.
>
> Someone died and you didn't get to say that last, fully present, goodbye. Family members celebrate a birthday, or the whole family celebrates a holiday, and you're not there because the Pacific's really big, and you're on the wrong side of it.
>
> Or your child can't remember her cousin's name, and she doesn't even know that's sad.

WORLDVIEW

Facing the subject of death and life beyond often brings out the definition of one's "worldview." Some individuals and cultures see death as final with no existence beyond. Others think that following death one is simply in a spirit world quite different than our own, which interacts with ours. Still others view life after death as a paradise existence that is very similar to our own, but unimaginablys better. Many hold to the concept that a judgment or evaluation of one's life follows death and that either reward or condemnation awaits each person who dies. A large number of the world's cultures and religions hold that a person immediately faces God in some way upon their death.

I have noticed that it is not uncommon for the bereaved to default to what their worldview is only to have questions about it. If they request it at this point, you can take the opportunity to help them answer and adjust their worldview where they have confusion. However, unless asked, you will be the most help to them by addressing their pain of loss.

But being aware of one's worldview can help you choose what to say. If they believe that death is the end of existence comments like, "Your loved one is in a better place." will be of no comfort. However, a comment such as, "Your loved one has no more pain." may help more.

RELIGION

Worldview is often influenced by religion. Understanding a griever's religious views can be a big help in your knowing what to say, or not. The beliefs of the Eastern Orthodox and Roman Catholic churches, for example, hold that the state or even future of a departed soul can be affected by intercessory prayers. Comforting folks who cling to this hope for their lost friend or relative can be more effective by you emphasizing the bereaved person's current pain and not saying things about the state of the departed.

Other religions such as the Jehovah's Witnesses and Seventh Day Adventists, view the state of the deceased to be in a form of unconsciousness until some future resurrection. Many Judeo-Christians believe the departed is instantly transported to the presence of God in a "heavenly" state of paradise. In making comments to these folks about their one lost, you should be politely aware of these beliefs. Again, remember that your role is to aid them in processing their grief and not to change their religious beliefs unless they specifically ask for your opinions on the subject of life after death.

Members of Islam believe that any form of suffering, including grieving, is a result of the griever's sins in some way. Their Prophet Muhammad declared: "By the One in whose hand is my soul (i.e. God), no believer is stricken with fatigue, exhaustion, worry, or grief, but God will forgive him for some of his sins thereby — even a thorn which pricks him." (Musnad Ahmad, You-Tube) So, you may aid such a person with words of assurance that will help them deal with guilt that may be unjustified. Physically showing grief with the bereaved would be in order, however, Islam discourages very loud crying and wailing at funerals. During the mourning time after a death, mourners expect to have visitors. Be sure to pay a physical visit to your Muslim friend within days following their loss.

In the case of Buddhism and Hinduism, the deceased is believed to be on a path to being re-born again in another physical life. Helping such a one cope with their grief could revolve around assisting them celebrate their loved one's life. Emphasizing the accomplishments and good traits in the form of scrapbooks and photo displays can bring inner comfort to the griever.

WHY?

The "Why?" question is a common expression when anyone experiences a loss. Whether it is the loss of a job or the loss of a child in a custody case, the "Why?" issue can creep in, or crash in. The emotional hurt from the loss can make a logical answer seem irrelevant.

When that question does loom over the griever, be slow to assume you have an answer. Remember, the one grieving is experiencing an emotional hurt and a logical reply may not be of help. They mostly need you to identify their pain and support them at this time. Don't play God.

Genuine concern goes a long way in helping the bereaved. Sensing your authentic caring is more help to them than a long prepared speech. Polite awareness of their worldview or religious persuasion will be helpful in aiding their grief.

◈

« Point to Ponder »

Comments that imply a judgmental nature are of no comfort to the bereaved.

WHAT TO SAY

WHAT NOT TO SAY

- ✓ **I was shocked to hear of your loss. I'm a friend who cares.**

    - ✗ *You must feel as bad as I did when.....*

- ✓ **I am so sorry for your loss.**

    - ✗ *Just stay busy and you will get by.*

- ✓ **Tell me about him/her.**

    - ✗ *You must stop crying. You might upset someone.*

- ✓ **I feel so sad for you.**

    - ✗ *You must be strong for others.*

- ✓ **What is something I can do for you this week?**

    - ✗ *He/she must have brought this upon himself/herself.*

"No one ever told me that grief felt so like fear."

C. S. LEWIS

Chapter 10

—

WHEN YOU GRIEVE

Tips for those who
are experiencing loss

I didn't know a human could hurt that much.

The hole in my soul was huge and indescribable after Ruth died. No one had ever taught me how to mourn or even what to expect. Of course, mourning was not high on my 'things to learn' list. Like many, I avoided it as some sort of weakness I didn't want anything to do with. The various "stages" I went through were surprises to me which often caught me off guard. I eventually had the presence of mind to seek out others who had gone through similar loss to talk about my experiences and pain. It really helped me understand and process my journey.

The previous chapters have been meant to help those who are aiding the bereaved with information and suggestions. However, I want to offer some suggestions here directly to those who are grieving.

UNDERSTANDING THE PROCESS

Although many authors have tried to categorize the grieving process, it really can't be done to perfection. I notice that any list of "stages" or experiences in print may not all apply to every person. Each person mourns a bit differently. However, just because one comes across something that does not apply to their situation they should not discount being made aware of the many options one may experience.

In an article published in *Tabletalk Magazine* entitled "Mourning with Those Who Mourn" Dr. Archie Parrish explains mourning:

> **Mourning** is one of life's universal experiences. To mourn means to feel deep grief, sorrow, heartache, anguish, angst, pain, misery, unhappiness, and woe. It is the opposite of joy. Mourning comes from loss that is perceived as irreversible, such as death, terminal illness, and devastating accidents. It is not expressed in the same way in every culture, but no matter where you live on the planet, sooner or later you will face 'a time to mourn.' In spite of the fact that all human beings mourn, each person's experience of grief is always unique. (2007)

HOW IT FEELS

If you feel like you are losing your grip on reality, you might be a perfectly sane person enduring the confusion of grief.

Perhaps you suffer irrational fear, dread or even paranoia. You may feel empty or numb like you are in shock. Grief even causes some people to experience trembling, nausea, breathing difficulty, muscle weakness, loss of appetite or insomnia. Feelings of anger can also surface, even if there is nothing in particular to be angry about. Almost everyone tortures themselves with guilt by asking what they did wrong, how they might have prevented the loss, or some other form of self-condemnation. In short, grief makes us feel like our emotions have gone haywire because, in many ways, they have. Over time, however, you will regain a measure of equilibrium.

DIFFERENCES

Having twice mourned the loss of a spouse, I have noticed that I even went through the process differently each time. There were similarities, of course, but the order and severity of some of my experiences differed.

Changes that affected my mourning journeys included the following:

- My level of maturity. I was 41 the first time and 63 the second.
- My knowledge of the mourning process. I was inexperienced the first time.
- The definition of the relationship lost. Ruth and I came from similar backgrounds and grew up together as adults. Judith and I came from different backgrounds and brought years of adulthood into the relationship.

- The level of my life-demands. The first time I still had children at home. The second time I came home to an empty house.
- The amount of mental and emotional preparation for the impending death. Ruth and I never really talked about her death. Judith and I mourned her death together and openly.
- The support group available to me. The first time I only had friends and coworkers near, whereas the second time I had 15 adult kids and spouses to hug me along the way.
- The depth of my faith. I surely had grown in my faith over the years.
- My willingness to embrace the pain. The first time I tended to try to avoid it in the early days.
- My willingness to talk about it. This became a key in both instances to my healing process.

A PROCESS, NOT AN EVENT

My personality tends to be a "fixer." Consequently, I found it difficult to accept the fact that grieving is a process and not an event. I wanted to do something and get it over with. That is no more possible than it is to put a cast on a broken leg one day and have it completely healed the next. Both take time. Time and pain became my constant companions. Grieving has no quick fix.

I also felt obligated to be strong and right at all times. It was a challenge for me to realize that my deep, erroneous opinion that mourning was a weakness or even a sin, needed to change. It would have been better for me early in my journey had I believed that grieving is normal and necessary for emotional and physical health. Through searching for relief of my inner pain, I did find others who helped me know that for the deepest, long-term healing I needed to "embrace" the pain fully. I liken it to a festering sore that needs continuous draining till complete healing has occurred.

PHYSICAL ASPECTS

One of the people in my support group circle was a nurse. Early on she gave me counsel on points to help my sleeping. At first I didn't know why she even suggested that, but soon I realized why. This was a bigger issue for me after Judith's death. It took me months to return to somewhat of a normal sleeping pattern. Being intentional about taking care of my health had been overshadowed by taking care of my wife. I needed to change that and begin considering my own health. Research has proven the grieving process to be a physical condition as well as an emotional one. To ignore this would be jeopardizing one's health. Stories abound of grievers who themselves experienced a physical decline in their health within two years of the loss of someone close to them such as a spouse.

I intentionally made goals to develop a regular time to go to bed, schedule in deliberate exercise, and to pay attention to eating balanced, regular meals. There were benefits to these and the results gave me sparks of hope for the future when grief tried to steal it. Slowly I began to feel the renewing of energy, which mourning had robbed from me. My weight began to return to a safer level. Others noticed, which encouraged me. After experiencing death so closely, it was uplifting to feel so alive again.

One of the wise things I did was to schedule a doctor's visit shortly after my wife's funeral for a checkup and advice. This was helpful to me in as much as I openly acknowledged the physical part of grieving and received some good pointers from the doctor as well.

DESPAIR VS. PURPOSE

The feeling of despair during grief could easily drag my thinking and feelings down. To combat this, I found it necessary to intentionally, and daily find and cling to purposes for my life. It was easy to let the grieving process define and totally control me. After Ruth's death I still had four teens in the house to care for and guide. My job at the college soon continued and speaking engagements began to come in. However, I still had to choose to see those events as meaningful purposes for my life in order to overshadow the periods of despair when blindsided by grief.

Many grievers have shared with me that they found diversion from their own despair when they reached out to help others. I also found that to be true. During Judith's decline and after her death, I found my concern for how my children and grandchildren were processing their own sorrow as a helpful release from my own despair in bouts of grief. Others have orchestrated grief relief groups, while still others volunteer at the hospital or retirement centers.

NORMAL QUESTIONS

"Am I going crazy?" "Why am I so tired all the time?" "Who really cares about me now?" "Why can't I think clearly anymore?" "Why is it so hard to make decisions?" "Will this ever end?" "Why am I the one that is still alive?" "Why has everyone forgotten my loved one?" "Why has everyone pulled away from me?" "What if I had handled things differently?"

If you find yourself asking any of the above questions you are going through a normal experience in the grieving process. Grieving requires a huge amount of physical and emotional energy. It is draining. You are the focal person who is experiencing grief in a concerted way. Your friends and relatives have gone back to their lives; that dominates their attention. It does not mean they have forgotten you or your loved one. In fact, often times they will mourn longer than you because they are so distracted with life that they only mourn in short remembrances and therefore spread out their mourning process over a longer period of time.

RELEASE THROUGH EXPRESSION

Many of my friends have said they were hesitant to bring up the subject of my grief and my wife because "they didn't want to make me feel bad or cry." Of course, what many don't realize is that talking about things can't make my grief worse. It helps to release it. So, in essence they were thinking about their own comfort. You can, therefore, help them and yourself by bringing up your journey and memories of your loved one. A friend who had gone through the loss of his wife while in a leadership position like me offered some wise advice. He said, "You need to embrace the process of grief. Don't avoid or stuff it. Your objective is to be healed and whole on the other side."

ABANDONMENT

The sense of abandonment crept over me as I experienced the loneliness that swelled up on every side. Without realizing it, I began to associate my feelings of abandonment from my wife's death to my friends and coworkers. Soon, thoughts that no one really cared about me any more opened up doubts about my social associations. This gave way to ideas of having to find new friends and even coworkers. It is true that a couple of friends pulled away from me because our relationship was primarily through my wife. However, transferring my sense of abandonment to my friends and coworkers was unfounded and misdirected. It became important to me to realize that my feelings of abandonment came from the loss of the intimate relationship I had with my wife. It left a big hole.

THE FIRSTS

As soon as my wife died, I began the process of experiencing all the "firsts" in life for me. The first time I talked to someone after she died. The first time I showed up in a familiar public place as a widower. The first time I went out with friends as a single. The first time I broke down emotionally in public. The first time I talked to someone who didn't know my wife died though her passing had been weeks or months before. The first time of going through each major holiday without her. The first time any anniversary came around. The first season change without her to enjoy it with. The first family gathering other than her funeral and she was not there. The first time I got news of a friend or event and she was not there to tell it to.

There is no best way to experience these "firsts" in life. I handled them in different ways. Some of them I literally "leaned" into by making a point to "get it over with." One of those "firsts" was the family gatherings without Judith. I purposely made it a point to go see my relatives even though I knew it would be difficult. Some of the holidays, however, I tended to avoid a bit by doing something totally different the first time after my wife died. The Christmas after Ruth died I accepted an invitation to join a friend for a special holiday out of the country. However, for the Christmas day after Judith died, I stayed home alone in the morning and cried most of that time. Then, in the afternoon, I joined in a community potluck and enjoyed it.

As I said before, a very important first for me was the first time I had a conversation with a stranger and did not feel like I had to make sure they knew I was recently widowed. That helped show me the grieving process does not always have to define who I am. So not all "firsts" are negative and hard. Some of the firsts can be steps in the direction of healing and freedom from deep pain.

You may find it helpful to identify your firsts. Please keep in mind that often these firsts are difficult for your friends and relatives as well as for you. Getting past them can be points in your journey of grief that will lead to victory.

HEAD-BASED VS. HEART-BASED

One of the potential grieving methods I found could be called "head-based vs. heart-based" grieving. The head-based part would be during times when I would use simple logic to deal with my loss. "She's in a better place." "I am strong and can get through this." "I know things will get better for me." The use of head knowledge and reason has its place. In fact, studies show that many men often use this style of mourning quite successfully. They tend to act or do something in memory of their loved one that "makes sense" in their grieving days. If you find this style helpful, don't feel guilty about it.

The heart-based part of the grieving process is often what folks tend to expect. Studies again, show that this method is common among many women; however, many men include this in their mourning process as well. Guilt can creep in when sessions of "heart-based" grieving seem either excessive or totally lacking. These are times when your emotions seem out of control and all-consuming. The only thing that really matters to you is your own emotions and grieving. Your pain grips your very soul and swells up on the inside. It feels inconsolable at times.

I have examples during my mourning months where I was misunderstood because I demonstrated one or the other of these methods. During my first wife's loss I tended to only use the head-based style in public and kept my emotional outburst sessions to myself. Her father later told me that he thought I did not cry at all for her loss. He was relieved to learn differently.

In contrast, after Judith's death I had the freedom to weep openly at church social gatherings. A couple weeks later, one of the people of the church told a pastor that I was not handling the mourning process well and that I needed counseling.

I say all that to give you freedom to apply whichever method of grieving suits you and your personality — It is okay.

WAVES OF EMOTIONS

The emotional waves during my grieving periods did not always follow logic but were real nonetheless. I could be thinking about circumstances or people, when guilt, anger, relief, regret, stress and jealousy and the like would pop up in my heart in ways that did not necessarily make sense. Because emotions don't always follow reason, it can be disconcerting to deal with. Time, talking and identification are often aids in dealing with these feelings. Again, not everyone experiences all these emotions the same way. I am just admitting that I had at least short struggles with these.

Learning to cope with my emotions was a new experience for me. Not being known for open expression of feelings, I was suddenly thrust into a reality I had only observed in others. Writing down lessons I was learning through my pain helped me. Finding a safe place to express my emotions was another benefit I learned to seek after. Acceptance, expression and time can be some of your best approaches to dealing with your out-of-control emotions.

IDENTITY CRISIS

Connecting the grieving process to the adjustment of life without my wife helped me understand some of my aches. The day-to-day chores and role responsibilities changed. Suddenly I was doing EVERYTHING by myself, whereas before my wife and I shared what needed to be done. I had to not only do all I had been doing in our daily life routine, but now I had to do her's as well, which included regular communication with our large family. Developing a new routine I could cope with took time. I found it helpful to not make any other major decisions for a while, until I got used to her simply being gone.

Part of this adjustment was relearning who I was. I was no longer Ruth's or Judith's husband. I was now single; a different person but still me. So, in addition to the grief and loneliness, I was going through an identity crisis. This adjustment included simple things such as the style of music I had playing in the house, what type of movies I watched, how often I went out in the evenings and what social events I chose to attend. I took advantage of this time to sort some of our things in storage and reassess their value and relevance in my life with her gone.

BEING SINGLE AGAIN

Being single again and the struggle with loneliness became bigger hurdles than the deep mourning. The deep mourning and grief is understandable, and there's the hope it will subside. Being single again and lonely looked endless.

Much of our society revolves around couples. The majority of our friends were couples. The challenge for both those couples and me was to reach beyond viewing me as half of a couple, to seeing me as a whole single. It was quite the process before I was able to think of myself that way. For me to even have a conversation with someone and not be constantly referring to something about my wife was a battle.

LONELINESS

Loneliness was harder to cope with than grieving. At first I was lonely for Judith. I wanted HER back. I missed HER. As I worked through that sense of loss, a deeper empty feeling began to haunt me. I remembered this phase from my grief for Ruth (at about the six month point) and remembered thinking I was going crazy or something. I had come to grips with losing Ruth (and Judith) and wondered if that was okay, but at the same time I felt even more empty.

This general loneliness is hollow. There was no one who really noticed — or really cared if I came home at six or seven at night. If something unique happened in my day, I had no one to share it with. No one would call me after an important meeting to see how it went. I always came home to a silent house. I had no one close to validate my life or share it with and so on. It was this phase that drove me back to the Lord for answers. Missing Judith was logical and made sense. THIS felt hopeless.

SUPPORT GROUPS

A few weeks after Judith's death I was invited by a friend to go with him to a grief support group. At first I was resistant, thinking I had enough pain of my own without going to hear about other people's hurts. However, since the topic was on losing a spouse, I decided to go. The safety of being with others who were very understanding of my mourning process brought a sense of security to me. It helped me release some of the tension I was feeling. So, I recommend that you seek one out in your area and attend some of the sessions. A very reputable one I have found is called Grief Share.

THE LEGAL STUFF

Especially in the case of losing a spouse, the grieving process can be compounded by all the physical and legal matters that need to be tended to. It seems never-ending. Legal matters such as getting jointly-held property into my name only added to such things as changing names on jointly-held bank accounts. I had to change the beneficiary on my life insurance. Business and individual-held credit card accounts had to be adjusted. Auto and home insurance ownership had to be changed. Dentists' offices and other doctors' offices had to be notified so they would stop sending reminders of future appointments for my wife. I even had to make a new will for myself. If these matters are overwhelming, seek out a trusted family member or friend to help you with a list of to-dos in this regard.

One of the ways I "plowed" through the mourning process is by watching for signs of improvement from my deep despair. It took over two months of near-hopeless loss, pain and loneliness before I saw signs of relief. First, I was able to watch the slide show of Judith's life all the way through without sobbing. Then I found myself able to remember her outside the eulogy mode (only saying positive and glowing things about her). I was able to remember some of her weaknesses without feeling guilty about it. Then on the Sunday before Christmas I felt myself feeling frustrated with the "selfishness of mourning." Now, that is not a negative because mourning IS all about you and your loss AND it is RIGHT. But for me to feel that way, I realized that in order for me to see that perspective I had to be at least a step outside the bubble of mourning I was trapped in. It became a moment of self-encouragement.

LEAN ON OTHERS

After the third month of my grieving process I felt like I was getting life back together. I even resented people who implied or even outright said that I still had a ways to go before full emotional healing. Looking back now I can see that they were right.

Pastor Rick Warren of California gives wise counsel in his article, *"In a Season of Loss, You Need God's People:"*

> When you're going through a season of loss, you need not only the support of other people; you also need the perspective of other people. When you're in a season of loss, you don't see the whole picture, your pain

narrows your focus, and you need other people who can help you see the big picture. We need each other desperately in the season of loss.

After you release your grief, it's time to let other people minister to you. Let them help. Let them comfort. Let them offer suggestions. Let them sit with you and grieve with you. And don't be embarrassed about it! That is one of the reasons God created the Church. We are a family, and we are to care for each other.

PROFESSIONAL HELP

So, how do you know if all you're going through is the "normal" process or that you need professional help? Friends, relatives and other professionals can often give insight to that. Theresa Karn (April 27, 2013) provides some helpful signs to watch for. Signs that grief has become complicated and that someone needs professional help are:

- hyper-sensitivity to loss experiences
- restlessness, agitation and over-sensitivity
- intrusive anxiety about death regarding yourself or others
- rigid, ritualistic and compulsive behavior
- flattened feelings – no emotional expression
- fear of intimacy or impulsive relationships or a lack of basic self-care.

She goes on to recommend the book *Treatment of Complicated Mourning* by Therese A. Rando.

IT WILL HAPPEN

In the throes of deep grieving, there are times it seems like there is no bottom to the despair. Be encouraged that it will not always be so bad. Life will renew and you will laugh again.

Vice President Joe Biden is no stranger to grief. A week after he was first elected to the Senate in 1972, his wife and daughter were killed in a car accident. Then in May of 2015, his son died from brain cancer. MSN news reporter Ezra Klein reflected on Biden's losses and a speech he gave to the parents of fallen soldiers on May 25, 2012:

> In that 2012 speech, Biden talks about the constant weight of grief. "Just when you think, 'Maybe I'm going to make it,' you're riding down the road and you pass a field, and you see a flower and it reminds you. Or you hear a tune on the radio. Or you just look up in the night. You know, you think, 'Maybe I'm not going to make it, man.' Because you feel at that moment the way you felt the day you got the news.
>
> Biden doesn't end the speech easy. He doesn't say the grief ever goes away. He just says, eventually, it makes room for other things, too.

"There will come a day – I promise you, and your parents as well – when the thought of your son or daughter, or your husband or wife, brings a smile to your lips before it brings a tear to your eye," Biden says. "It will happen."

So, it will happen for you too.

◈

« Point to Ponder »

Beware of time in words of comfort. Avoid time limits and be sensitive to timing for comments.

GRIEF RESOURCES: It is not necessary to cope with your grief alone. Others have walked the path through loss and can help you understand your own pain. If you do not have access to a friend or professional to talk through your experience, I suggest you seek out assistance through other resources available to you. Use this link to find a variety of resources that can be of help to you regardless of what stage of mourning you find yourself in. http://bit.ly/1Ra2135

WHAT TO SAY

WHAT NOT TO SAY

✓ **Your heart break must go deep.**

    ✗ *You need to be alone when you grieve.*

✓ **It breaks my heart to see you in such pain.**

    ✗ *You need to stop feeling bad/crying.*

✓ **I'm sure you cherish your time with him/her.**

    ✗ *Don't burden others with your feelings.*

✓ **How have you been feeling this week?**

    ✗ *He/she is with God now.*

✓ **Is today a better day for you?**

    ✗ *All things must pass. Time will heal.*

"Sorrows cannot all be explained away in a life truly lived, grief and loss accumulate like possessions."

STEFAN KANFER

Chapter 11

—

WHEN THE NOT-SO-UNUSUAL HAPPENS

Helping others with losses of pets, jobs and divorce

The meeting was well-attended. I talked for over 45 minutes on areas of my life affected and lessons learned from grieving the loss of two wives. In the course of my discussion I gave a list of other experiences in life where grieving often needs to take place. Among them was the loss of a cherished pet. I specifically made the statement that, "It is okay to grieve!" in such situations.

She sat on the aisle seat in the very back row. As I exited the auditorium my route took me right past this middle-aged lady sitting alone. Approaching her location, I noticed tears in her undecorated eyes as she handed me a note and whispered, "Thank you." It read: "Thank you for your kind words. No one thinks of us who lose beloved pets. These pets are our children too! No one in the (community) helps us to grieve. They say kind words for the moment and then they forget. We who lose them do not forget their love to us. We are told to move on. Angel died three years ago, July 2. She was my Baby Girl. I mourn her still. The sorrow is with me still. Thank you again for your kind words." (Lauren)

PERMISSION TO GRIEVE

The permission I gave that day for her to grieve brought a release and victory over her pain long overdue. The insensitivity of friends, and her erroneous thought that she should not feel that way over the loss of an animal, had caused turmoil within her for a long time. Freedom felt good to her.

Today's society of electronically connected and busy people produces more and more individuals who experience lonely existences. To compensate, in part, many have invited a pet into their lives at a very emotionally close level. As these pets die their owners mourn them like they would any family member. This has gotten so prevalent that in the United Kingdom the PBSS was established a couple of decades ago as a joint venture between the charity Blue Cross and the Society for Companion Animal Studies. Primarily by phone, this agency offers emotional support to those who call in after losing a beloved pet.

BROWNIE

My own attachment to pets began with Brownie, a pet ewe sheep my grandfather gave me at age seven. Brownie was the very first pet that was mine, all mine. I would go to the pasture and just watch her graze. Seeing her in the barn lot gave me a warm feeling. Late that first winter Brownie was due to give birth. My mom had grown up around her dad's flock of sheep so she knew a few things about the lambing process. One day Mom announced that Brownie was sick with something that can accompany pregnancy in sheep. The regular checks on her began.

Then it happened. Mom went out to check on Brownie just after she tucked me into bed. Before I was sound asleep she came back into my room to gently announce that Brownie had died. I said, "Okay," and she left the room. My room was small but had a high ceiling and I was in a three-quarter sized bed all by myself. I remember rehearsing over and over in my mind, "Brownie is dead. Brownie is dead." Shortly my mom came back in to find my eyes filled with tears. "I was afraid of that happening," she responded. Her gentle voice and soft strokes on my back helped calm my broken heart.

LADY

Following my dad's death when I was eleven years of age and the eldest of five, an uncle gave us a Dalmatian dog. We did not have her very long before circumstances made it necessary that we sell her. Soon after that a neighbor offered our family a puppy from a mixed-breed dog they had. Mom let me pick which one I would like. I named her Lady. I would have to say myself that she was so ugly she was cute. Distinct characteristics from all three breeds in her lineage showed up in unusual ways.

During my high school years Lady became my sidekick and friend. We lived at that time on the edge of a small Iowa town, which was barely one-mile square in size. I often went to town to see cousins, mow lawns and generally "hang out." Any time I left our small acreage on the outskirts of town Lady went with me. Everyone in town knew I was in town if they saw Lady. It was not uncommon for me to go into the front of a store and then exit out the back leaving Lady waiting at the front for me. She would wait for half a day on several occasions before giving up and going home.

For me, springtime is great in southern Iowa, as everything comes to life. The spring of my senior year in high school wasn't so pleasant, however. Following a phone call, my step-dad found me in the garden with some bad news. Lady had been hit by a car and was in really bad shape. He felt I should be the one to take care of it. I got our old pickup and went to the scene of the accident. They were right. She was fatally wounded. I knew what needed to be done. I took her to a very remote area of our farm and "put her down." I stood there with an ache in my heart. Tears were not common for me, but they coursed down my cheek that sunny afternoon.

The next day I told a friend about the sad incident. I remember that I felt a lot better telling her. I also remember how much she empathized with me.

SUGAR BEAR

Years later, our family had another pet. This time I was an adult with three young children of my own. Sugar Bear was a medium-sized dog with a great nature. He had been trained as a protector of small children. Our family inherited him as a gift from the previous owners. Soon our kids were attached to him.

We were living in a densely-populated neighborhood. One of the neighbors south of our place had a big dog that was not very pleasant. The dog matched the nature of his owner. When my kids were outside with Sugar Bear we were careful to keep him close.

One summer day the inevitable happened. The neighbor was out with her dog and so was Sugar Bear. Soon, Sugar Bear could stand it no more. He became convinced that dog was a threat to my kids. He ran across the lawn and attacked the larger dog with vigor. Foolishly, the neighbor jumped in between the fighting dogs to break it up. She emerged with tooth marks and declared that they were from Sugar Bear. Not satisfied, she took it a step further and complained to the authorities.

The situation escalated to the point that finding a new home for Sugar Bear was the best option. It was a sad day in the Knapp household.

Unfortunately, the lessons I had learned about the value and need of grieving the loss of a pet as a teenager failed to show through me that day. When I told my daughter the news, she began to cry. My immediate response was to shush her up and force her not to cry. I now believe that was an improper thing to do. An understanding hug and a soft voice of empathy — like my mom did for me — would have been better.

GRIEVING LOSS

Pets can be very important companions. Emotional attachments can run nearly as deep as those with other humans. The loss of those relationships (with pets) can cause just as deep a hole in one's spirit as losing a close relative or friend. Forbidding a friend or relative to grieve the loss of a pet can cause them unnecessarily extended pain.

When talking to someone who has lost a pet, the best thing to do is to acknowledge their pain. You may not be comfortable being concerned about the departed pet's welfare, but the pain of the owner is real. Let them express their hurts. Listen for however many months (or years) it takes for them to be victorious over their pain. Their grieving process is just as real and necessary as any other loss.

In her blog post (April 21, 2010) entitled "Mourning the Death of a Pet," Tara Parker-Pope cites statistics that substantiate this connection:

> Last year, researchers from the University of Hawaii's animal science department conducted a study to determine the level of grief and stress when a pet dies. Among 106 pet owners interviewed from a veterinary clinic, 52 percent had lost one or more pets from natural causes, while 37 percent had lost a pet to euthanasia. Although many pet

owners experience significant grief when a pet dies, about 30 percent reported grief that lasted six months or longer. Severe grief that resulted in major life disruption was less common but was estimated as high as 12 percent of those studied.

A FAILED MARRIAGE

The number of divorces in our society today continues to be on the rise and has become commonplace. Just because it has become commonplace doesn't mean it is any easier to work through. I have observed many who stuff down or overlook grieving as part of processing their loss.

My first close experience with divorce was that of my mom and step-dad. As with many marriage failures, theirs did not happen overnight. The decline of their relationship occurred slowly over a period of time.

In addition to the disagreements my folks had, there were other signs that they were experiencing a breakdown in their marriage relationship. Increasingly my step-dad would find reasons to be gone out of the house for longer periods of time. At the same time I saw my mom pull out old pictures of my father, whom she had not successfully grieved for, and look at them in tears. I believe that she mistakenly identified her present pain, which was a form of grief, with her unresolved grief over her first husband.

GRIEVING OVERLOOKED

Loss through divorce is huge, yet often overlooked. It is overlooked by those involved in the divorce because life goes on without an actual death. It is overlooked by friends because the relationship breakdown is not usually sudden and often viewed as "their fault, so let them deal with it."

The effects of unresolved grieving over a divorce can extend for years when it is not viewed as a "grievable loss." The losses that need to be addressed can vary from reputation to dreams. One friend wrote, "The thing I've been grieving most so far hasn't yet been the loss of my wife/lover, but more so the loss of my teammate, and the loss of my kid's mother."

You can be a helpful friend to one you know has experienced a divorce by lovingly discussing these often overlooked areas of loss. This will aid them in working through the grief caused by divorce.

HOW LONG?

One of the fundamental differences between grieving the loss of a marriage relationship through divorce and losing it due to death is the closure issue. When death occurs, the closure is a certain and final. With a divorce the grieving process can be much longer, depending on the contact that occurs after the breakup (as in child custody).

The error of ignoring any grieving when a family is broken due to divorce can be harmful. Of course, the process will vary, as with all grieving, due to the circumstances and individuals involved. But the option and even requirement for grieving this loss (and failure) can be easily overlooked.

In cases where loss is predictable, the grieving process can be a part of one's experience even before divorce papers are final. Other cases tend to be more of a surprise, or hope is held onto till the end. Grieving can then be more intense after the papers are filed.

FEAR AND ISOLATION

In the grieving process, fear and isolation often go together. The griever often feels fear while the rest of their circle of friends responds by isolating them till they "get over it." However, potential comforters are too often hampered in helping the hurting due to their own fears. They are afraid to talk to them because they "don't know what to say" and are therefore afraid they will say the wrong thing.

Whether it is your fear or the fear of the one who has experienced a loss, beware of the tendency of isolation. Many mourners have expressed that when they needed to talk about "what happened" and the relationship they lost, most of their friends pulled away and seemed afraid to talk about it.

Be the one to break the cycle of fear and isolation in someone's grieving process. Bravely step up to the plate with a listening ear and thoughtful question that will give the griever freedom to openly discuss their loss.

GRIEF LETTERS

Grief letters can often be very helpful in processing a loss. Those who have faced the devastation of a marriage ending, as well as those who have lost their job or pet, can each find help by writing a letter describing their deepest hurts. Though the letter is not directed to a specific person, neither is it beneficial solely to the mourner. Reading it can help friends and family to better understand the pain being experienced.

The idea of writing a "grief letter" may seem trite to many who have not experienced loss, but I and my family have found it helpful in releasing pain. I wrote such a letter to the leadership of the religious non-profit organization from which I was released. There was more ease of my pain resulting from writing the letter than I experienced in receiving the generic letter they sent in response. And as I mentioned before, but it bears repeating — I saw the relief from pain my daughter experienced after writing a letter to her mom a couple months after her death.

JOB LOSS

Many college graduates never work in the field of study in which they receive a degree. I am not among that group. I found a deep sense of fulfillment in finding a career about which I was passionate from the start. I served with a religious non-profit organization that was very team-oriented.

On one of our first encounters with the leadership of this group their deep heart-felt convictions and passion showed through. I remember turning to my wife, Ruth, and asking her, "So, do you think you could spend the rest of your life working with people like that?" Through her tears she mumbled, "Yes!"

Following our year-and-one-half of orientation and leadership training, we were assigned to a teaching and leadership position. The next eight years saw the addition of our four children and the privilege of working in partnership with other veteran leaders. The opportunity to become closely associated with new candidates who came through the training facility deepened our roots in the organization further than anything I had ever experienced in my life. Indeed, we became closer to many of our co-workers than we were with many family members.

My next assignment was to teach and serve as president at a junior-college-level training school in another state. We moved and quickly settled into our new roles there. With loyalty as one of my personal character strengths, my commitment to the job given to me ran deep. Our family life revolved around the work I did at the school.

Then tragedy struck. Cancer. During those seven years of battling cancer together as a family, I plowed through the personal stress it forced on me and whole-heartedly continued my roles at the school, only asking for breaks to take Ruth to her doctor appointments. I did this right up to the day she died.

Two years after Ruth's death I married again. Judith and I each had four teenagers to bring into the marriage. The only issue our marriage created revolved around a policy of the organization that all members take a one-year orientation training like the one I taught at for my first eight years with them. Judith had not received this training before we were married.

This policy had been "law" with this organization since its inception. None of the leaders at that time had the freedom (nerve) to make exceptions. The "pink slip" came in the form of a decision that for us to continue with the group, we would have to resign from the school, move our family to another state and attend this training program as students — actions that were logistically impossible for our family. We were effectively OUT of the organization.

LOYALTY OVERRULED

I remember that difficult day. One of the leaders came into my office and began with, "Dave, this is very hard for me to say." My entire insides seemed to begin aching all at once. I was stunned, hurt and felt totally abandoned by people whom I thought to be my friends. My heart was so wounded I did not even say anything in my defense. I WAS OUT. I had not done anything wrong.

My strong sense of loyalty prevented me from showing my pain and rejection. I defended the leadership and stuffed my grief very deep. I never shed a tear. I simply wrestled with my grief in my soul and my thoughts.

Following the fulfillment of our responsibilities with that school we moved our family across the USA to begin a new life in a new community at a new job. I was working two jobs and blending eight teenagers. Needless to say, busyness often prevented time for reflection.

Judith was the only person who really knew I was a hurting guy. My kids noticed I had become more "quiet" at our meal table. A co-worker at the new school commented that I did not seem to be the leader/outgoing guy he would have expected from a former president of a college. My spirit was indeed hampered by my repressed grief.

The loss of my job and the position I served in for 14 years was the second most difficult loss I had ever experienced. Only losing my first wife, Ruth, was harder up to that time. I did not deal with this grieving process well. It extended for three years.

Finally, however, I gained victory through coming to grips with the grieving and releasing it. I was alone on our property with some livestock we owned. I suddenly burst into tears and sobbed for the longest time as I remembered some of my close friends who were still with that organization who "let me go." They were able to continue carrying out the passion for that work we both shared. I had been deprived of that. I was forced out against my will. One final thing I did that helped me was to write a grief letter to some of the leadership team involved. Doing so provided a measure of freedom to my spirit.

I have heard many other examples where men who lost their jobs went into deep depression for a long time. Like me, these men often found their personal identity in their work. When that is lost, they flounder for identity and security. Since many men seem to think mourning is not "manly," they try to tough it out instead of grieving freely for victory.

One thing that might have been helpful to me during those three years of grief would have been for someone to open the subject of my job loss and ask me how I got through it or what it was like going through that loss emotionally. Even asking me how I felt the day I was "let go" may have opened the topic for my heart to be expressed and freed from some pain.

WOMEN IN JOB LOSS

Experiencing grief due to the loss of a job is not gender-specific. It may be true that men tend to attach their identity to their job, while women tend to find security from their job; however, the loss can be just as traumatic for either.

Crystal realized that her loss of a job caused depression brought on by her grief. She began sleeping late and not even dressing to go out for the day. Those who helped her most were friends who tuned into her experience through caring. One friend called her each morning for awhile to encourage her to get out of bed and face a new day. Crystal soon began getting up and dressing as if she were going to work. This lightened her spirits and helped her work through the deep hollow feelings of loss.

Not all of her friends were as understanding. One, whom she visited shortly after her job loss, did not factor her grief into her less-than-perky actions and criticized her "lack of caring." This can be a challenge to all of us to be sensitive and give allowances to friends we know who face losses in the normal course of life, like losing a job.

« Point to Ponder »

Sympathy for the griever by recognizing their present pain has more value than attempts to empathize by comparing to your past losses.

WHAT TO SAY

WHAT NOT TO SAY

✓ **I'm not sure what to say but I want you to know I care.**

    ✗ *You will find another to replace them.*

✓ **I can't fix your hurts but I can be here for you.**

    ✗ *You can't fall apart.*

✓ **Can I call you to chat on Saturday evening?**

    ✗ *"What is done, is done," I always say.*

✓ **I am so sorry this is happening to you.**

    ✗ *This is a blessing in disguise.*

✓ **We have missed you lately.**

    ✗ *I have had a bigger loss then you so I know it is not as bad as it could be.*

*"Grief is not a disorder, a disease or a sign of weakness.
It is an emotional, physical and spiritual necessity,
the price you pay for love. The only cure for grief is to grieve."*

EARL GROLLMAN

Chapter 12

—

WHEN I GRIEVED SUCCESSFULLY

How I found strength and wisdom
to survive loss and do it well

"**I** don't know how you do it. You have lost two wives and you seem to be doing so well," came the familiar statements. Following Judith's death many people made similar comments to me. Some remarks came as simple observations while other people were genuinely seeking answers.

In this chapter I will be taking the liberty to lay out the thinking process and worldview I have developed in the course of my life and freely explain how that all affected my grieving process. My family background, personal experiences, logic, religious beliefs and the message of the Bible all come into play to determine how I approached and responded to tragedy. It has been my observation that most people default to these things when they hurt.

My earnest prayer is that the truths laid out will be a help to you as you face your own losses, and as you help those who come across your path who are hurting from loss.

THE BIBLE

It was a blessing from God and huge privilege to be born into a strong family who had a deep belief in God based on His Word, the Bible. I didn't do anything special to be born where I was. However, the mindset, beliefs and teachings of my family and church were fundamental in establishing my worldview of life and death. The family heritage I acquired held to an established belief in the God of the Bible that went back several generations on both sides of my family. I not only heard the message of the Bible from my parents but from my grandparents and aunts and uncles as well.

CHOICES

So, if family and the geographical location in which one is born are vital in how one processes grief, why is it that not everyone who has these benefits processes grief well? Because included in the mix are the personal choices of each individual. Simply being exposed to a belief system, whether through family or by culture, is only the beginning. Your personal choices and convictions are what activate those teachings and messages.

THE NEED

The core truth of the Bible that my mom taught me revolved around God creating man to have a close relationship with Him. As the Creator of the universe, God chose to only have this personal relationship with mankind. Since God represents and *is* everything just and good, a relationship with Him had to revolve around what He is like. The first man created, Adam, broke that bond by doing something contrary to God. He disobeyed a command, consequently breaking the created relationship between God and mankind. Since He is everything just and good, God set forth a plan to fix the broken relationship. He promised this plan and then executed it by sending Jesus, His Son, to live a perfect life among men and women and then die, making the restoration of that relationship with God the Father possible. He decided it would be a gift to be received by faith. Anyone who rejected God's plan through Jesus would spend eternity after they died separated from God.

My mom showed me places in the Bible that clearly explained this. Thankfully, she also made it clear that I was required to make a choice about God's gift through Jesus for myself. She pointed out that my core relationship with God wasn't broken just because I was a bad boy once in a while, but that I needed to respond to God's message because I was born needing it. She read to me from the Bible, "Therefore, as through one man's offense judgment came to all men, resulting in condemnation..." (Romans 5.18). Adam's "offense" was passed on to every human born thereafter, making a personal response by each individual a requirement. Not believing in God's plan for restoration seals the judgment. "He who believes in Him [Jesus] is not condemned; but he who does not believe is condemned already, because he has not believed in the name of the only begotten Son of God" (John 3.18).

THE PROVISION

As a child, I enjoyed Christmas as much as any other kid. We were humble economically and I remember times when there was only a single gift for each of us. However, Mom and my church teamed up to help me see a bigger picture. Christmas was the celebration of the coming of Jesus to earth in order to accomplish God's plan to restore mankind to a right relationship with Him. I enjoyed hearing the stories of Jesus' life in my Sunday school classes at church. They explained that the purpose for Jesus becoming a man was for Him to die for the wrongs things performed by all mankind. "… that Christ died for our sins according to the Scriptures, and that He was buried, and that He rose again the third day according to the Scriptures, and that He was seen of Cephas, then by the twelve" (1 Corinthians 15.3-5). We can know that God, in turn, accepted the work of Jesus' death as payment for all our violations of God's nature because He raised Him from the dead. "… God … promised before through His prophets in the Holy Scriptures, concerning His Son Jesus Christ our Lord, … and declared to be the Son of God with power according to the Spirit of holiness, by the resurrection from the dead" (Romans 1.1-4).

MY FIRST RESPONSE

My mom read the Bible to my brother and me every night she could before we went to bed. When I was seven years old, she told us one night that the Billy Graham Crusade was on TV and that if we were good while she read the Bible we could stay up a little longer and listen to the music part. Well, I wasn't so good and was sent to bed. While my brother watched the music, I was in bed alone, thinking. Mom came in and found me crying. "I don't want to go to hell when I die," I blurted out through my tears. Mom reviewed again that all I needed to do was believe on Jesus for myself and God would restore my relationship with Him and that Jesus' death and resurrection would pay for all my wrongs against Him. I did that. I knew from that time on that upon my physical death, I would spend all of eternity in the presence of God the Father. I would go to heaven.

THE EVIL

The problem with the evil in my heart had been resolved before God, to be sure. It didn't mean that I didn't still blow it from time to time. Mom knew that for sure! However, she was faithful to continue to expand my knowledge about evil in the world we live in. She told me the story about Satan and how he rebelled against God. He was then confined to earth and now takes his vengeance out against God on mankind. He uses evil to resist God and God's people. Teachers at church taught me that because I was one of God's children, Satan would target me for harm and evil intentions. However, I don't have to be defeated by him but be aware that sometimes when bad things happen it may be coming from him. I can win over his intentions with Jesus. "You are of God, little children, and have overcome them, because He who is in you is greater than he who is in the world" (I John 4.4). "Therefore submit to God. Resist the devil and he will flee from you. Draw near to God and He will draw near to you" (James 4.7, 8).

My instruction about evil continued. Because of Satan's rebellion against God and the disobedience of Adam to God's commands, evil has a strong influence on the earth and the world as we know it. This evil curse affects all of God's creation, including mankind. The negative things caused by evil include such things as weeds in my garden, weather that is destructive, immorality, murders, mistreatment of people, bad intentions and responses to one another, and disease. Until the day Jesus returns and corrects all of that, we can expect evil to continue. Evil, therefore, can happen to us simply because we are humans living in this world at this time. Bad things can happen to good people for no fault of their own.

MY EXAMPLE

My seven-year-old mind had a lot of questions about what it is really like to live one's life and have a personal relationship with God. This is where my family and church friends came in again. I watched how they did it. The two people closest to me who demonstrated evidences of having a personal relationship with Jesus were my mom and her mother, my grandmother.

Regardless of any character or personality flaws in them that I may have observed over the years as I grew up, those ladies proved to me that it was possible for Jesus to be a personal friend. When they talked about Jesus, I could tell He was not an abstract concept or a theory of religion. He was a real person to whom they talked and listened often.

My mom's connection to God was consistent. She would go to Him during times of hurt, such as when my dad died or we had severe financial difficulties. She would sing to Him when she was happy in good times. Her example showed me that I could do that too. And I did.

MORE CHOICES

My high school years were times of change for our family. Mom remarried and three more sisters were added to our family. The family blending process was not always an easy one for me, being the oldest child. We also moved, I went through puberty, and attended a high school in another town. I chose to remain consistent in following the Biblical mindset of God as the sovereign of the universe and Lord of my life through all these changes. Church was a core part of my life. I enjoyed hearing teaching from the Bible, singing songs and hymns about God, following Him, and looking forward to being with Him in heaven someday.

The summer between my junior and senior year presented me with another life-changing choice. I had been offered a scholarship to a leading agricultural university in Iowa. I knew I needed to pray about it, so after church one evening I stopped at a pasture near our farm buildings where I prayed often. God spoke back to me saying, "Follow Me." He indicated that I was to prepare to officially be in a position to do things that would promote His message in the world. I said, "Yes." The following week I received a catalog in the mail from a Bible college in Kansas City, Missouri. I chose to turn down the scholarship and applied to the Bible college instead. I knew that my life was being directed personally by God and I trusted Him.

My choices were made based on my friendship with Christ. I believed what He said in the Bible. "Greater love has no one than this, than to lay down one's life for his friends. You are My friends if you do whatever I command you. No longer do I call you servants, for a servant does not know what his master is doing; but I have called you friends, for all things that I heard from My Father I have made known to you" (John 15.13-15).

FAITH CHALLENGED

My years studying at the Bible college were very formidable. As I increased in knowing what the Bible says and what it means, I developed a desire to know my Friend better. Trusting Jesus more and walking by faith became major personal goals. I aspired to the definition of faith in God that the Apostle Paul spoke about. "First, I thank my God through Jesus Christ for you all, that your faith is spoken of throughout the whole world" (Romans 1.8).

Soon, I began to realize that to "walk by faith" included more than just major choices. It involved how I went about my day-to-day living. Simple statements began having a deep impact on my approach to daily living. A quote of unknown origin I have never forgotten is, "If you were arrested for being a follower of Jesus, would there be enough evidence to convict you?" Jesus said, "And why do you call me, Lord, Lord, and not do the things which I say?" (Luke 6.46)

Based on my personal relationship with Jesus, faith and faithfulness became daily goals in my life. Though much of my daily life was laid out for me — class and work schedules, job responsibilities, class requirements and sleeping — I began to realize that I chose much of how I lived my life. I chose my responses to situations, my attitude towards people and circumstances; I chose how I spent my money, what social functions I attended and how well I used my discretionary time during waking hours. I began to see that my proper or improper response to errors and mistakes I made was based on whether I was responding out of faith in God or my selfish desires. Even though my learning curve seemed huge, I willingly climbed it towards a closer relationship with God.

LIFE GOES ON

Following my college years, life progressed somewhat "normally" (whatever that is). I got married, received a job assignment, had children, developed friendships, increased in responsibility both at work and home, and so on. My wife, Ruth, and I were on a "normal" course in life, building a career and raising a family of four. We practiced the lessons learned in trusting God and living in close relationship with Him in all areas of our life as best we could. We trusted Him in our finances, parenting, free time, friendships, job roles and church attendance. He was always faithful. We took to heart, "... whether you eat or drink, or whatever you do, do all to the glory of God" (1 Corinthians 10.31).

My reference to life being "normal" includes ups and downs in life that happen to all of us. It includes mistakes by each of us in our family. Disappointments that come financially, professionally and socially are all integral to our human experience.

IN CRISIS

Cancer is not what is usually considered normal. I have heard it said that "anyone can trust God when things are going good." But do we really trust Him when it doesn't seem like we need Him that much?

We had no clue to what depths the downward spiral would lead us when Ruth announced that she had found a lump and should make an appointment with an oncologist. The following weeks and months were full of challenges, hurts, disappointments and even low-level mourning.

The lump was an aggressive form of cancer. Treatments included surgeries, chemotherapy, radiation and constant testing.

Yet, our hope continued to be secure, based on our relationship with God. Though we desired the security of pain-free life, we trusted Him more. Believing that pain was a part of human experience and that we were not exempt from it helped us overcome the bouts of "why me?" and unfounded feelings of "being punished."

Our friend Jesus never left us during our down times. We knew that because He said so. "For He Himself has said, 'I will never leave you nor forsake you.' So we may boldly say: The Lord is my helper; I will not fear. What can man do to me?" (Hebrews 13.5, 6).

It was true that going through a crisis like cancer was a new thing for us. We had never experienced such a hard thing before. However, trusting Jesus in our lives was nothing new and so we kept doing that. We simply needed to learn how to go through this hard thing. Our pain and tears were always met with the comfort of our personal relationship with Jesus Himself.

THE REALIZATION

Trusting God during our hard times did not keep us from sometimes struggling with our questions.

One afternoon following severe chemotherapy treatments, Ruth was on the phone with her mother. Ruth asked the "Why me?" question to her mom. Louise's response was classic. "Well, Ruthie, why not you? Up to now your life has been pretty simple and pain free. Why do you think you should be exempt from hard situations and others not?" This, of course, agreed with what Jesus Himself said, "In the world you will have tribulation; but be of good cheer, I have overcome the world" (John 16.33).

Ruth was a nurse. She had seen many, many people in the

hospitals she worked in going through all kinds of physical pain and sufferings. She knew that her mom was right about many other people experiencing physical crisis, of all ages and walks of life. It is all a part of living in this world that has so much influence from evil. Pain and suffering does seem to be a normal part of human experience. Each of us somehow hopes it won't happen to us.

DEATH

I had never seen anyone die before. Watching Ruth take her last breath was shocking. All I could think about was that she actually died! She was gone. My heart immediately began to hurt in ways I had never experienced before. Grief encompassed me, suffocating me.

My first response to God was again based on my relationship with Him up to that time. I called out to Him as a friend for help with my hurt. I did not lash out at Him as a distant tyrant in the sky who "did this to me." He had helped me learn how to handle so many things in my life so far, I knew He would help me with this grief. And He did.

I would go to the Bible for words of assurance and comfort in times of hurt. Over the years, since I received so many encouraging messages from God's Word, I knew I could count on my Friend to have words of comfort and purpose as well. I was not disappointed. "Blessed be the God and Father of our Lord Jesus Christ, the Father of mercies and God of all comfort, who comforts us in all our tribulations, that we may be able to comfort those who are in any trouble, with the comfort with which we ourselves are comforted by God" (2 Corinthians 1.3, 4).

Ruth's cancer and death were not a result of her sin, but a "normal" result of living in a world that is affected by the influence of sin. Just because we had a relationship with God on a spiritual level did not exempt us from the regular operation of nature and genetics. God simply has promised to help us through experiences in life. We trusted Him for a bigger picture.

BIGGER PICTURE

We remembered the account in the Bible where Jesus was asked who had sinned, causing a man to be blind from birth. He replied, "Neither this man nor his parents sinned, but that the works of God should be revealed in him" (John 9.3). Jesus went on to heal that man that day.

Ruth's death was not a defeat. She actually won. You see, she had the privilege of going to heaven into the very presence of God without the hassle of living here in a world influenced by evil for the next forty or so years. Even though I was left with the hole in my soul grieving, I had the privilege of seeing God use my loss to show others how He comforts in uncommon ways. A bigger purpose was realized. Many people have been helped in their journey through life in this evil world because of our story.

I remember one such example of this. A local pastor stopped me in a public elevator. He said, "I hope you didn't mind me using you as an illustration in my sermon on

Sunday." I looked surprised but indicated that I was sure it was okay. He went on to explain. "I read your recent letter about your wife's illness. I liked your perspective. My point to the congregation was to show how a follower of Jesus should handle pain and suffering based on a relationship with Christ. You have shown us how it's done." I was humbled.

NEW BEGINNING

Judith and I shared the same Biblical worldview. During our courtship time we spent hours reviewing our common experiences of going through the process of suffering and the death of our spouses. We both had learned how to deal with pain and death from God's Word and our personal relationship with Jesus. We were on the same page.

Having a common worldview and relationship with Jesus was paramount in the development of our unity in dealing with the challenges of life we faced together in the twenty years that followed. Blending and finishing raising eight teenagers did indeed have challenges. Many times we had no place to turn to other than each other and God when times got tough.

Judith's physical concerns during the last five years of her life left many questions in our minds, but none of them shook our trust in God's leading and care. God had been so consistent in giving inner peace and direction to us in so many areas over the years, that we had no reason to question Him now. We were faithful to walk in the truth we came across whether it had to do with nutrition or spiritual dependency on God.

DEATH AGAIN

That day in the hospital when I told Judith she was going to die soon is etched in my memory. We held each other and sobbed deeply for a long time. We mourned her death together for several days. Our assurance of God's leading, care and closeness did not eliminate our pain of impending loss. But it did provide a basis for how we faced the months ahead.

The weeks before Judith's death provided many opportunities to talk to family and friends about her "home going" and how God factors in. Anyone talking to her during those weeks needed to be comfortable with the topic of life after death because she talked about it freely. Many people were helped with their viewpoint on Christians going to heaven and how to view that event by Judith's conversations. I found a statement in Judith's notes that reflected her attitude. "God can get just as much glory from a sick body as He can from a well one."

Relief, instead of shock, crossed my mind at Judith's death. She had suffered with a lot of pain at the end – and now her pain was over. But then an overwhelming grief hit me, producing uncontrollable sobbing. I hurt.

PRAYER

Prayer can play a huge part in the grieving process. Telling the bereaved that you are praying for them can be of great comfort. It was for me. My heart ached so bad at times that I found even praying difficult if not impossible. Comfort crept in as I remembered all the people who I knew were praying for me. God gave me added assurance that not only were these people praying *for* me, but they were praying *on my behalf* or literally in my place. This news increased my peace and freedom to embrace grief fully.

LONELINESS

Following Ruth's death I still had four kids at home to care for and I was still teaching at the college. My struggle with loneliness had to take a back seat many days, oftentimes showing up at night. However, after Judith's memorial service I went home to an empty bed and an empty house. The phone stopped ringing because everyone knew she was gone. Visitors to the door dwindled to maybe a couple a week. I found myself wandering around the house only to find another empty room. The loneliness and silence was deafening. I had never experienced such aloneness before in my life.

Per my personal practice, I turned to God and His Word for some help and guidance. I begged God to show me how to cope with the stifling void.

His answer came to me from the Gospel of John in the Bible which I had also read following Ruth's death. This record reveals points about the last weeks of Jesus' time and teaching on earth before He went back to His Father in heaven. I began to see a pattern in the things He said to the Apostles. "Little children, I shall be with you a little longer" (13.33). "Where I am going you cannot follow Me now, but you shall follow Me afterward" (13.36). "I go to prepare a place for you" (14.2).

"These things I have spoken to you while being present with you" (14.25). "But now I go away to Him who sent Me..." (16.5). Jesus was talking about His departure to heaven and leaving the disciples alone on earth. Everything He said in between these statements was instructions on how to deal with the loneliness.

LONELINESS INTO GODLINESS

I found a series of guidelines from Jesus Himself concerning things I could do to deal with and even take advantage of my loneliness. I noticed that Jesus did not instruct to simply sit around and "suck it up." He proceeded with guidelines and commands that increased my relationship with God and literally helped me be more like Him.

His directives in the Gospel of John were basic but clear:

1. Depend on one another (13.34)
2. Stick with your core beliefs (14.1)
3. Remember what you know about heaven (14.2)
4. Don't forget about My return (14.3)
5. I am the Way to true life (14.4-6)
6. Remember My words (14.10-12)
7. You can have success (14.12)
8. Pray (14.13-14)
9. Obey My commands (14.15, 21, 23)
10. The Holy Spirit will help you (14.16-18)
11. Loneliness can help you (14.19, 26)
12. Embrace My peace (14.27)
13. Give God glory (14.13; 16.14; 17.1, 4)
14. Keep close to Me (15:1-8)

Each of these items was significant to me. Some helped my thinking clear up. Others eased the torment of my emotions. I would need to write a chapter per item to explain all of them clearly. That will be left to be covered in another book and another time.

To illustrate, however, I will review number three: heaven. Jesus talked about it as if it was a real place He was going to and promised I could be there too someday. That reality reduced some of my fear of the unknown about where my loved ones were after death. It also gave me peace about *my* future since my death, someday, was as sure as their death. My mental worries about the "after-life" relaxed and my emotional concerns regarding my loved ones were soothed. Hence, my grief was processed more calmly.

YOU

To put my conclusion very bluntly, I know my world-view *works* because of my lifetime of experience based on God and His Word. It is with great confidence I can offer this information to you.

The fact that you have read all this till now indicates an interest on your part in the message I am communicating. I sincerely hope and pray that something I have said here can be a help to you. Also, if you do not currently have the right relationship with God I have referred to above, I would like to invite you to begin that now. "For God so loved the world [you] that He gave His only begotten Son, that whoever [you] believes in Him should not perish but have everlasting life. For

God did not send His Son into the world to condemn the world, but that the world though Him might be saved" (John 3.16, 17).

◆

« Point to Ponder »

When you stand before God at your death and He asks you, "Why should I let you into My heaven?" what will be your answer?

RECOMMENDED BOOK:
The information in this chapter summarizes much of the material and topics from the Bible. Now it is time to increase your understanding of God's plan. Please use the link below to obtain your copy of a book (youth or adult) that simplifies God's plan for us to an easy-to-grasp story.
http://griefreliefministries.com/resources/

WHAT TO SAY

WHAT NOT TO SAY

✓ **May God bless you and give you strength and comfort.**

> ✗ *If you had more faith, he/she would not have died.*

✓ **What do you need most today?**

> ✗ *God does not give us more than we can handle.*

✓ **What would you like to say to him/her right now?**

> ✗ *You need to forget about him/her and move on.*

✓ **You must be hurting deeply.**

> ✗ *He/she is in a better place now.*

✓ **God mourns with those who mourn.**

> ✗ *It is too soon to face your grief.*

"How do you pick up the threads of an old life? How do you go on?
In your heart you begin to understand. There is no going back.
There are some things time cannot mend.
Some hurts have gone too deep...that have taken hold."

MR. FRODO,
The Lord of the Rings:
The Return of the King

Chapter 13

—

WHEN TO DO WHAT

Timeline suggestions for
practical things to do to help grievers

E very circumstance is different when people experience loss. Each individual grieves differently. Some people spread their mourning process out over a long period of time while others seem to be very concerted in their grief. Generally speaking, there seems to be similar patterns in the process that can help us understand what to do at different times to be helpful.

The following schedule is the one I tended to follow during my grieving process for both my wives. In no way am I implying everyone should follow this exact pattern, but my journey can serve as a working example of loss.

AT DEATH

The day each of my wives died I was fortunate to have friends or family present. I can't imagine not having them there. My wives' deaths left me so numb that I could not even think straight for a while. Having someone there, even if they said nothing, helped me function. They took care of the daily logistics of physical things like meals, cleaning, and decisions that needed immediate attention.

Don't wait or even expect someone to ask for your help at the death of their loved one. They may not be able to even make that simple of a decision. Seek out ways to help by visiting or calling.

THE FIRST WEEK

This time period gets foggy for many grievers. The possible decisions required can be overwhelming. Everything from finding a funeral home to choosing a casket to planning and executing a funeral become monumental things to deal with — and that on top of grief. This week can be very stressful for the individual as well as the family. Even the best of families can have conflict over some of the details that are required at this time. Many of these things are often handled by the family members nearby, but sometimes that is not the case.

Making yourself available to help with the planning for the events of this week can be a first step. Because grievers often have trouble thinking clearly, gentle suggestions as to things that need to be handled and an offer to help can be in order. The little details such as transporting flowers from the memorial service to the cemetery can be on your list of offers to help. Meals for the bereaved and their guests are often a huge blessing during this week. If there is a funeral or memorial service, make every effort to be there. A phone call every couple of days is often appreciated to remind the bereaved that they are not alone in their pain.

THREE WEEKS

Phone calls, sympathy cards and references to my wives took a noticeable decline at about the third week. It seemed like someone made a public announcement and the whole world said, "That's it. We will forget her now."

For me, however, the opposite was happening. The numbness had subsided enough that the reality of her absence was finally reaching my foggy brain. I was permanently alone again now. My need to talk about the whole event increased instead of reduced. My deep emotional sobbing sessions had gone from three times a day to one or two. My mind needed to process what my emotions had seemingly been responding to. I needed to talk about her death more than ever. I remember thinking that I would have given anything to have someone ask me, "How did your wife die? Tell me about it."

Many people would ask me, "How are you doing?" I would answer, "Fine." However, the ones that helped me the most would be more specific with, "How has this week been?"

or "Tell me where you are in your journey or recovery process."

I remember being stricken with the fear that everyone would forget her. I was clinging to memories of her, but it seemed everyone else was forgetting. So, I did things to ensure a recorded legacy for each of my wives. For Ruth, I wrote an article for a Christian magazine about her life and got it published. For Judith, I asked my two daughters to each put together a photo book about her. One was a legacy book with pictures and information about her family. All eight of my kids' families were given a copy. The other was a "grandma" book of pictures of Judith and each of the grandkids, one kid per page. Each grandchild received a copy for Christmas that year.

A face-to-face, or at least a phone call, with the intent to talk a couple of hours about the loved one's death and the grieving process experienced by the bereaved should be offered. Avoid general statements when arranging this. Be specific with, "I would like to hear the details of how you are processing your pain and your recovery."

THREE MONTHS

Three months from my wives' deaths the grieving process seemed to release its grip on my emotions. I began to laugh again. I found myself more at ease in public alone. My sobbing sessions had subsided to one every other day. Still, from time to time I had to audibly tell myself that she really did die. The truth continued to sink in. However, I still hurt and felt like I had this visible "hole in my soul" as I lived life. I craved communication, intimacy with an adult, someone to talk to about my feelings. At this point, logic statements began to help more than just the heart comments that I needed before.

Long talks about my grieving process were harder to come by as most of my friends were expecting me to be "getting over it" by now. Finding someone who understood and would not "think ill" of me became harder to do. I set out to relieve this need by talking to other men who had lost a wife in recent years. That helped.

Your relationship with a bereaved friend may not be close enough for you to have conversations about "how are you feeling these days?" However, you could encourage them to have such a conversation with someone they know who would listen. Talking through one's process and progress can be a big step for them to realize and embrace the steps they have taken towards healing.

A card of encouragement to a bereaved person can assure them that you have not forgotten their pain and are supporting them in their progress towards victory. It can be an aid in helping them cope with their loneliness as well.

SIX MONTHS

I thought I was going crazy. It had been six months since my wife's death and many days I still felt as hollow and uncertain emotionally as I did the first month after she left. *What is wrong with me?* I mused. *Everyone thinks I am doing so well outwardly, but I still feel like something is missing on the inside.*

For me, the six month stage was kind of like the "teenage years" in my mourning process. I didn't feel quite like I was out of the woods (i.e. an adult) but I had progressed past the seemingly out-of-control emotional times (i.e. childhood) I experienced for so many months. My sobbing sessions were measured by the week instead of per day, and my interest in my future had increased.

At this stage I still had the need to talk to people who would be comfortable with me sharing deep feelings and with people who had been there, done that. One man I had such a talk with told me later that it was a bit uncomfortable for him, but it sure helped me. Another one stopped listening to me after a few minutes. So it obviously takes a special person to fill this bill.

Though I realized both my mental and emotional states were nearing a more victorious place of healing, "relapses" back to the ache stage were common. Assurances that my time in this "in-between" stage of the grieving process was normal would have been great comfort. If someone close to me had "given permission" for me to address the ache that came back periodically, I believe I would have been relieved of some guilt.

During my grieving experiences with my wives at this six-month time period, people "told" me that I was very vulnerable emotionally. My response was bewilderment and even anger. *I don't feel emotionally vulnerable,* I thought. *And besides, how do they know how I am emotionally? They haven't even talked to me about it.*

Caring words of caution from a trusted friend would have

been more effective than a casual acquaintance making a judgment from a distance. It's important to honestly assess one's level of relationship with the griever.

The truth is that I really was still emotionally vulnerable. I am thankful to God that I did not make any emotional decisions that I would have regretted later. I would not see that truth for another three months. At the nine-month period, when I looked back at how I was feeling in comparison, I realized that my emotional state had improved and I felt "more like myself." The possible decisions I could have made during the most tumultuous grieving, both socially and in my career, would not have lined up with my lifetime personal core values.

NINE MONTHS

Much counsel has been given in our culture to not make any major decisions for twelve months following losing a spouse. In many ways, I see the wisdom for that. It provides opportunity to go through one cycle of life dealing with all the "firsts" after losing a mate. For the griever, time is your friend. In the case for both my wives' deaths, I had grieved in a very concerted fashion. I had "leaned into" my pain and embraced grieving willingly. Not everyone does that, I guess.

For me, the ninth month of grieving was a turning point. I finally felt very secure socially. I felt like my emotions were more "normal." Remembering my wives did not cause pain or emptiness. I even enjoyed it when friends teased me about finding another wife sometime. I considered re-marriage more seriously.

This stage varies with people, for sure. I have known of some men who were at this point after six months of grieving, while some women I have met have admitted it wasn't until the eighteen-month time frame that they were open to give their hearts away again in romance.

BIRTHDAYS, ANNIVERSARIES, HOLIDAYS

Among the important "firsts" grievers go through are the first holidays. For some these times can be nearly as difficult to experience as the day the loved one died. Cards, phone calls and even invitations to do something special can be put on your schedule on behalf of the bereaved person.

The first Christmas after Ruth died my family and I appreciated an invitation by a friend to spend the potentially difficult holiday in a location we had never been to before. The first Christmas after Judith died I responded to an invitation to attend a community-wide potluck dinner and thoroughly enjoyed myself.

Remembering wedding and death anniversaries with a card, phone call or visit can help the bereaved cope with the day because someone besides them remembered. They feel less lonely due to the fact you shared it with them. Even responding in some way at the deceased's birthday can have the same effect.

TWELVE MONTHS

The one-year mark for grievers tends to carry an uncertainty with it. How will they feel the day of the anniversary of their loved one's death? Will anyone else remember? What should they do that day to commemorate their loved one, if anything? You can come alongside to help with many of these questions.

Be mindful of the possibility that the anniversary can be a significant event for years to come. Many, not only rehearse about the one that they lost, but also the grief associated with that loss.

A phone call or card showing you remember your friend and their loved one will go a long way in bringing comfort. If possible, you can also do something physical with them. Take them out for coffee or dinner and talk about the life of the deceased. Going with them to visit the cemetery and bringing flowers in memory of their loved one will help establish a bit more closure and peace to the bereaved.

I have known of a few good friends and close relatives who have taken the effort to put some of the above suggestions on their yearly calendar and actually follow through with them. Believe me, if you don't make yourself a note in some way you will most likely forget.

◆

« Point to Ponder »

Knowing the right thing to say is only half of the responsibility of being a supportive emotional care giver. The other half revolves around the doing.

FREE SCHEDULE: Wanting to help someone over the long term and remembering to do it can be two different things! I have put together a handy spreadsheet schedule you can use to remember ways to aid the griever for the first year following their loss. Click on the following link to get your copy. http://bit.ly/1COXuxg

Being a Better Friend to Those Who Experience Loss

WHAT TO SAY

WHAT NOT TO SAY

✓ **He/she was full of life. I remember the time when….**

    ✕ *You'll get over this soon.*

✓ **I have been praying for you since his/her death.**

    ✕ *Let me know how I can help sometime.*

✓ **Where would you say you are in the grieving process?**

    ✕ *At least now you can put this behind you and get on with your life.*

✓ **(3 months later) Tell me about your journey so far.**

    ✕ *You have no right to be angry at God.*

✓ **(6 months later) Tell me about your journey so far.**

    ✕ *He/she has been dead for a while now. Aren't you over them yet?*

"The first duty of love is to listen."

PAUL TILLICH

Chapter 14

—

CONCLUSION

Making a difference in your world
by being a better friend

Grief is indeed a difficult subject to face. For most of us it does not attract our attention as a topic that we naturally wish to be an expert on. Yet, coping with loss qualifies as a natural part of life. Because you have read this book, you are ahead of many of your peers and relatives in your ability to deal with grieving.

Knowing what to say, or not say, often comes through a better understanding of the grieving process. Such understanding does not always have to be obtained through personal experience. We can benefit from that of others willing to be honest about their feelings and journey following a loss.

Hopefully the experiences and observations collected in this book have increased your awareness of the grieving process. You are now more skillfully equipped to be a better friend to those around you who experience loss. Most of us will encounter at least one person within the next year who will be called on to process some sort of loss. It may even be you.

IN REVIEW

Comments of comfort should not be geared to "fix" the problem of grief for the bereaved. Commonly, too many who have not dealt with the mourning process will attempt to avoid it when faced with the grief of others. Grief cannot be fixed, it needs to be processed. So, the first thing we can do is to acknowledge the pain instead of trying to make it go away fast.

Grief is the acknowledgement of loss emotionally. It is mostly a heart problem, not a mind challenge. Heart statements go farther in comforting the bereaved than head statements early on. Logically explaining away grief does little in soothing the hurt in the heart. Mind logic can play a part in long-term processing of loss but it comes up short when the most encompassing pain at the moment is emotional.

Mourners are sensitive to unsupportive comments that seem to minimize their grief. Grieving comes from deep within us. Denying it or diminishing it can be perceived as a personal criticism. Such implications may cause guilt and withdrawal on the part of the grieving and be a hindrance to their ability to process their loss victoriously. Allowing them to grieve will uphold them better.

Avoiding grievers socially, or avoiding the topic of their loss, stifles their grieving process. Grief can become the proverbial "elephant in the room" with grievers. They feel it even more than their friends. Excluding them from social events and conversations only accentuates their pain. Avoidance does not soften the pain for them. To eliminate the topic of their grieving experience and the one they have lost is to ignore the most important thing that is happening in their life. Good friends don't do that.

Avoid time limits. Setting a time limit on how and how long any one person is allowed to grieve over a particular loss can be demeaning to the griever. They can feel like you are being disrespectful towards their loss or loved one. Be aware of timing in words of comfort. You need to be discerning in knowing when to make certain comments to a griever. Being a better friend revolves around listening and supporting their journey, instead of limiting it.

The grieving are not looking for logic statements of being told what to do. What they need is a listening ear. No one likes to be "bossed" around under the best of circumstances. To "command" a person who is grieving in an attempt to "talk them out of it" may only drive them away from you as a person with no effective help to their pain. Instructive statements must be well-timed and presented in the form of suggestions or examples. Grievers need to be heard more than directed.

Theological lectures are seldom of much relief for the pain of new grief. Theological arguments at the time of loss can be misconstrued as a rebuke. This can come across as rejection and not a form of comfort. Religious beliefs are often embraced in the mind through the logic door. Emotional pain is seldom soothed deeply through that avenue. Again, timing can be very important if this topic needs to be addressed.

Consolation for the bereaved needs to be more about their personal pain, than about the one they have lost. The temptation is very strong to talk more about the person or item lost, than about the needs of the griever. The deepest problem is the emotional pain inside. Logical statements about the person or items lost can be of help. However, if we ignore the heartache being experienced, we will not help our friend to work through their journey as effectively.

Comments that might be interpreted as a judgmental attitude are of no comfort to the bereaved. No one likes to be told they are wrong or at fault for the loss. The bereaved commonly cope with forms of guilt in the normal flow of the process. It is no help to add blame to their pain. They are at a very vulnerable time in their lives and your words must be chosen carefully.

It is common for the supporting friend to feel a certain amount of discomfort but this shouldn't be a hindrance. Remember that your words of comfort need to revolve around the feelings of the bereaved. Many of the "What Not to Say" comments were blurted out by would-be comforters uneasy with their own feelings. It's helpful to stay away from statements that begin with, "I always say" and "you should just" to grievers. Keep your attention on the emotional state of your friend.

Recognizing the griever's present pain has more value than attempts to empathize by comparing to your past losses. The tendency to "one up" on a griever in an effort to sympathize with them usually results in a comparison game that can diminish the pain of the griever. Also, since each person grieves differently, it is not usually beneficial to make comparisons but simply to seek understanding of the mourner's experience.

Knowing the right thing to say is only half of the responsibility of being a supportive emotional caregiver. The other half revolves around the doing. I am truly grateful to the people in my life who not only knew what to say but followed through with the supportive action. Many of my friends and family were active the day and weeks following the death of each of my wives. Others called me months later asking to go for a walk and talk, or go out to eat. My family openly talked with each other and me about their mom's memories and how much they missed her. I was asked often by acquaintances to speak publicly about my grieving journey.

THE REST OF THE STORY

Life goes on. Mine has indeed progressed in fine style. The evidence that I have "practiced what I preach" about the mourning process becomes apparent with the developments in my life beyond my grieving period. I am living proof that the suggestions you have read in this book work and have merit.

I documented the points of progress in the grieving and healing process by writing a "progress report" to my children. This public diary served as a teaching tool for the family on grief and a victory record for me.

The following year after Judith's death, after much re-definition of who I am, my emotions and focus in life began to settle to a new level. My vision to write this book was established. I received a refreshed job description in my career work. I moved out of the house where Judith died. With help from one of my daughters, I established a profile on Christian Mingle.

Each of the new, solid developments in my life was possible because my emotions had been given clear and ample time to grieve fully by my "leaning into" the process and having those around me who gave me permission to do so with their support.

Many of these changes have given me a new, full and purposeful life. First of all, I met Crystal Wacker. What a lady! She has entered my life with love and wit that brightens every day. Our marriage has completed my life at a whole new level. Her support for me in life's challenges and accomplishments has been invaluable. In addition to her continued work as editor of *Reach Up* Magazine, she helps me in my writing and speaking engagements.

I'm confident that through the information in this book you have gained some insight on how to be a better friend to a griever. And I encourage you to make a difference in the lives of friends who have experienced loss. If you wish to share this material with a greater circle of influence, I am available to speak for conferences, meetings and employee training.

Acknowledgements

Writing this book was bittersweet emotionally for me. I needed to spread it out over a long period of time due to the emotional stress I experienced in order to recall and express clearly what my grieving was like. Thanks to so many of my friends who just kept encouraging me over the months of labor to press on and stressed the high value the information will be to so many people.

Writing the book was only part of the process. The editing and actual production of this book required a circle of dedicated people whom I wish to acknowledge. Becky Norwood has been invaluable in the execution of promotion and publication. Plus, I want to express a heart-felt thanks to those who have been such a help in the editing process. Thanks to Steve and Cindy Wright, Kathy Gibbens, Rosie Cochran and Rhonda Brown for their thoughtful and professional input.

My kids and grandchildren have been fabulous throughout the losses we have experienced together and their dedicated support of me and my efforts to get our story in print. I love you all.

A special note of love and appreciation goes to my wife, Crystal Wacker Knapp, who has been my biggest cheerleader of late and who has put in so much effort in the editorial process. Thanks Doll.

Bibliography

Aldrich, Sandra. *Living Through the Loss of Someone You Love.* Ventura: Regal Books, 1990.

Athan, Lisa. "Don't Say to a Griever..." *Grief Speaks* Blog, October 2014, available at http://www.griefspeaks.com.

Drakeford, John W. *Holman Bible Dictionary.* Nashville: Broadman & Holman, 1991.

Elliot, Elizabeth. *Loneliness.* Nashville: Thomas Nelson, 1988.

Garfinkl, Perry. "Men in Grief Seek Others Who Mourn." *New York Times*, July 25, 2011.

Groves, Elizabeth W.D. *Becoming a Widow.* Greensboro: New Growth Press, 2012.

Haugk, Kenneth C. *Don't Sing Songs to a Heavy Heart.* St Louis: Stephen Ministries, 2004.

"How to Help a Bereaved Parent." WikiHow, May 2014, available at http://www.wikihow.com.

James, John W. and Russell Friedman. *The Grief Recovery Handbook.* New York: Harper Collins, 1998.

Kaplan, Robbie Miller. *How to Say it When You Don't Know What to Say*. New York: Penguin Group USA, 2004.

Karn, Theresa. "If You Are Grieving The Loss of a Spouse, Here are Some Approaches to Help You Heal." Carizon Family and Community Services, April 27, 2013.

Klein, Ezra. "Joe Biden's 2012 Advice to Grieving Families is All the More Poignant Now." May 31, 2015, available at http://www.msn.com/en-us/news/politics/joe-bidens-2012-advice-to-grieving-families-is-all-the-more-poignant-now/ar-BBkrnXo?ocid=SKY2DHP.

Konigsberg, Ruth Davis. "5 Surprising Truths About Grief." *AARP*, March 14, 2011.

The Maxwell Leadership Bible: New King James Version. John C. Maxwell, Executive Editor. Nashville: Thomas Nelson, 1982.

Means, James E. *A Tearful Celebration*. Portland: Multnomah Press, 1985.

Mourning Matters Ministry, Spring 2013.

O'Rourke, Meghan and Leeat Granek. "How to Help Friends in Mourning." August 4, 2011, available at http://www.meghanorourke.net.

Parker-Pope, Tara. "Mourning the Death of a Pet." *New York Times*, April 21, 2010. available at http://well.blogs.nytimes.com/?module=BlogMain&action=Click&region=Header&pgtype=Blogs&version=Blog Post.

Parkins, Daniel. *Nineteen Days*. Mustang: Tate Publishing, 2013.

Parrish, Archie. "Mourn with Those Who Mourn." *Tabletalk magazine,* 2007.

Price, Tabitha Joy. *Joy Comes in the Mourning.* Mustang: Tate Publishing, 2012.

Rapp, Emily. "What Not to Say to a Grieving Parent." Role Reboot, February 20, 2013. available at http://www.rolereboot. org/life/details/2013-02-what-not-to-say-to-a-grieving-parent.

Rohrer, Finlo. "How Much Can You Mourn a Pet?" *BBC News Magazine,* January 13, 2010. available at http://news.bbc.co.uk/2/hi/uk_news/magazine/8454288.stm.

Sandberg, Sheryl. Post on Facebook, June 3, 2015.available at https://www.facebook.com/sheryl/posts/10155617891025177:0

"Sex Differences in Prolactin Change During Mourning." *Journal of Psychosomatic Research.* 1987.

Sittser, Jerry. *A Grace Disguised.* Grand Rapids: Zondervan, 2004.

Swift, Joy. "How to Survive the Death of a Child." *Signs of the Times Magazine,* December 1987.

Trotter, Jonathan. "Outlawed Grief, a Curse Disguised." *A Life Overseas,* December 22, 2013 available at http://www. alifeoverseas.com/outlawed-grief-a-curse-disguised.

Van Ens, Jack R. "Visiting the Grief-stricken." *Ministry Magazine,* September 1987.

Warren, Kay interviewed by Morgan Timothy C. "Kay Warren: A Year of Grieving Dangerously." *Christianity Today,* March 28, 2014.

Warren, Rick. "In a Season of Loss, You Need God's People." Daily Hope with Rick Warren, May 21, 2014.available at http://rickwarren.org/devotional/english/in-a-season-of-loss-you-need-god-s-people.

Wiles, Tiana and Jeremy. "Sex before Marriage Rewires Your Brain." May 13, 2015. available at http://www.charismanews.com/culture/49599-sex-before-marriage-rewires-your-brain.

Wintz, Susan and Earl Cooper. *Cultural & Spiritual Sensitivity – A Learning Module for Health Care Professionals*. New York: HealthCare Chaplaincy, 2009.

Wortman, Camille, Ph.D. "Offering Support to the Bereaved: What Not to Say." *This Emotional Life* Blog, October 2014, available at http://www.pbs.org.

Young, Ed, Ph.D. "7 Things Not to Say to a Grieving Person." May 2014, available at http://www.crosswalk.com.

"Your Journey From Mourning to Joy" Grief Share, Wake Forest: Church Initiative, 2006.

Moving Forward

Because David Knapp is passionate about helping as many people as possible with the material contained in this book, he offers himself to anyone who deals with people regularly as well as the rest of us who interact with friends and family.

As a capable speaker and communicator, David Knapp is available to do public presentations and seminars – keynote, half-day, or full-day – for various venues and audiences.

To book an appointment call (866)-596-0470 or go to the website: http://griefreliefministries.com/speaking-engagements/

Other ways to connect with David are:

twitter.com/david_knapp1
facebook.com/griefreliefmin
youtube.com/griefreliefministry
linkedin.com/in/griefreliefministries